ACHIEVING OUR COUNTRY

The William E. Massey Sr. Lectures in the
History of American Civilization

1997

RICHARD RORTY

ACHIEVING OUR COUNTRY

Leftist Thought in Twentieth-Century America

Harvard University Press
Cambridge, Massachusetts
London, England

Library of Congress Cataloging-in-Publication Data
Rorty, Richard.
Achieving our country: leftist thought in twentieth-century
America / Richard Rorty.
p.   cm.—(The William E. Massey, Sr. lectures in the history
of American civilization; 1997)
Includes index.
ISBN 0–674–00311–X (alk. paper)
1. Radicalism—United States—History.   2. Radicals—United
States—History.   3. Right and left (Political science)—History.
I. Title.   II. Series.
HN90.R3R636   1998
303.48´4—dc21
97–43210

Second printing, 1998

These lectures are dedicated to the memory of
Irving Howe and of A. Phillip Randolph, Jr. I had
only fleeting personal contact with these two men, but
their writings, their social roles, and their political
stances made a great impression on me when I was
young. They seemed then, and still seem,
to symbolize my country at its best.

CONTENTS

ACHIEVING OUR COUNTRY

AMERICAN NATIONAL PRIDE: WHITMAN AND DEWEY

NATIONAL PRIDE is to countries what self-respect is to individuals: a necessary condition for self-improvement. Too much national pride can produce bellicosity and imperialism, just as excessive self-respect can produce arrogance. But just as too little self-respect makes it difficult for a person to display moral courage, so insufficient national pride makes energetic and effective debate about national policy unlikely. Emotional involvement with one's country—feelings of intense shame or of glowing pride aroused by various parts of its history, and by various present-day national policies—is necessary if political deliberation is to be imaginative and productive. Such deliberation will probably not occur unless pride outweighs shame.

The need for this sort of involvement remains even for those who, like myself, hope that the United States of America will someday yield up sovereignty to what Tennyson called "the Parliament of Man, the Federation of the World." For such a federation will never come into existence unless the governments of the individual nation-states cooperate in setting it up, and unless the citizens of those nation-states take a certain amount of pride (even rueful and hesitant pride) in their governments' efforts to do so.

Those who hope to persuade a nation to exert itself need to remind their country of what it can take pride in as well as what it should be ashamed of. They must tell inspiring stories about episodes and figures in the nation's past—episodes and figures to which the country should remain true. Nations rely on artists and intellectuals to create images of, and to tell stories about, the national past. Competition for political leadership is in part a competition between differing stories about a nation's self-identity, and between differing symbols of its greatness.

In America, at the end of the twentieth century, few inspiring images and stories are being proffered. The only version of national pride encouraged by American popular culture is a simpleminded militaristic chauvinism. But such chauvinism is overshadowed by a widespread sense that national pride is no longer appropriate. In both popular and elite culture, most descriptions of what America will be like in the twenty-first century are written in tones either of self-mockery or of self-disgust.

Consider two recent novels: Neal Stephenson's *Snow Crash*, a bestseller, and Leslie Marmon Silko's *Almanac of the Dead*, a critical triumph which was not as widely read. Both are powerful novels. Readers of either may well think it absurd for Americans to continue to take pride in their country.

Snow Crash tells of a twenty-first-century America in which the needs of the entrepreneurs have won out over hopes of a free and egalitarian society. The country has been divided into small franchised enclaves, within each of which a single corporation—IBM, the Mafia, GenTech—holds the rights of high and low justice. The U.S. government has gone into business for itself and is one more corporate entity, running its own little enclaves. But the government is not even first among equals. There is no overall political entity, much less any sense of citizenship, that binds the eastern and western states together, or that links even the various districts of the big cities.

In *Snow Crash*, the relation of the United States to the rest of the world is symbolized by Stephenson's most frightening creation—what he calls the "Raft." This is an enormous agglomeration of floating hulks, drifting endlessly round and round the Pacific Rim, inhabited by millions of Asians who hope to jump ship and swim to North America. The Raft is a sort of vast international slum ruled by cruel and anarchic criminal gangs; it is quite different from the orderly franchises run by profitable business enterprises, respecting each others' boundaries and rights, in what used to be the United States of America. Pride in being an American citizen has been replaced by relief at being safer and better-fed than those on the Raft. Lincoln and Martin Luther King are no more present to the imagination of Stephenson's Americans than were Cromwell or Churchill to the imagination of the British whom Orwell described in his book 1984.

Snow Crash capitalizes on the widespread belief that giant corporations, and a shadowy behind-the-scenes government acting as an agent for the corporations, now make all the important decisions. This belief finds expression in popular thrillers like Richard Condon's *Manchurian Candidate* and *Winter Kills*, as well as in more ambitious works like Thomas Pynchon's *Vineland* and Norman Mailer's *Harlot's Ghost*. The view that the visible government is just a false front is a plausible extrapolation from the fact that we are living in a Second Gilded Age: even Mark Twain might have been startled by the shamelessness with which our politicians now sell themselves.[1]

Novels like Stephenson's, Condon's, and Pynchon's are novels not of social protest but rather of rueful acquiescence in the end of American hopes. Silko's *Almanac of the Dead* also assumes that democratic government has become a farce, but her novel is dominated by self-disgust rather than self-mockery. Its focus is on the relation of European-Americans to Native Americans and to the descendants of the slaves brought from Africa. Silko's novel ends with a vision in which the descendants of the European conquerors and immigrants are forced back to Europe, thereby fulfilling Native American prophecies that the whites would be a temporary disaster, a plague that would last no more than five hundred years. Silko portrays the American government collapsing amid riots and food shortages, as the descendants of the Maya and the Aztecs stream into California, Arizona, and Texas.

One does not need to know whether Silko has read Foucault or Heidegger to see her novel as offering a vision of recent history similar to the one which readers of those two philosophers often acquire. In this vision, the two-hundred-year history of the United States—indeed, the history of the European and American peoples since the Enlightenment—has been pervaded by hypocrisy and self-deception. Readers of Foucault often come away believing that no shackles have been broken in the past two hundred years: the harsh old chains have merely been replaced with slightly more comfortable ones. Heidegger describes America's success in blanketing the world with modern technology as the spread of a wasteland. Those who find Foucault and Heidegger convincing often view the United States of America as Silko does: as something we must hope will be replaced, as soon as possible, by something utterly different.

Such people find pride in American citizenship impossible, and vigorous participation in electoral politics pointless. They associate American patriotism with an endorsement of atrocities: the importation of African slaves, the slaughter of Native Americans, the rape of ancient forests, and the Vietnam War. Many of them think of national pride as appropriate only for chauvinists: for the sort of American who rejoices that America can still orchestrate something like the Gulf War, can still bring deadly force to bear whenever and wherever it chooses. When young intellectuals watch John Wayne war movies after reading Heidegger, Foucault, Stephenson, or Silko, they often become convinced that they live in a violent, inhuman, corrupt country. They begin to think of themselves as a saving remnant—as the happy few who have the insight to see through nationalist rhetoric to the ghastly reality of contemporary America. But this insight does not move them to formulate a legislative program, to join a political movement, or to share in a national hope.

The contrast between national hope and national self-mockery and self-disgust becomes vivid when one compares novels like *Snow Crash* and *Almanac of the Dead* with socialist novels of the first half of the century—books like *The Jungle*, *An American Tragedy*, and *The Grapes of Wrath*. The latter were written in the belief that the tone of the Gettysburg Address was absolutely right, but that our country would have to transform itself in order to fulfill Lincoln's hopes. Transformation would be needed because the rise of industrial capitalism had made the individualist rhetoric of America's first century obsolete.

The authors of these novels thought that this rhetoric should be replaced by one in which America is destined to become the first cooperative commonwealth, the first classless society. This America would be one in which income and wealth are equitably distributed, and in which the government ensures equality of opportunity as well as individual liberty. This new, quasi-communitarian rhetoric was at the heart of the Progressive Movement and the New Deal. It set the tone for the American Left during the first six decades of the twentieth century. Walt Whitman and John Dewey, as we shall see, did a great deal to shape this rhetoric.

The difference between early twentieth-century leftist intellectuals and the majority of their contemporary counterparts is the difference between agents and spectators. In the early decades of this century, when an intellectual stepped back from his or her country's history and looked at it through skeptical eyes, the chances were that he or she was about to propose a new political initiative. Henry Adams was, of course, the great exception—the great abstainer from politics. But William James thought that Adams' diagnosis of the First Gilded Age as a symptom of irreversible moral and political decline was merely perverse. James's pragmatist theory of truth was in part a reaction against the sort of detached spectatorship which Adams affected.

For James, disgust with American hypocrisy and self-deception was pointless unless accompanied by an effort to give America reason to be proud of itself in the future. The kind of proto-Heideggerian cultural pessimism which Adams cultivated seemed, to James, decadent and cowardly. "Democracy," James wrote, "is a kind of religion, and we are bound not to admit its failure. Faiths and utopias are the noblest exercise of human reason, and no one with a spark of reason in him will sit down fatalistically before the croaker's picture."[2]

In 1909, at the beginning of his book *The Promise of American Life*, Herbert Croly echoed James:

> The faith of Americans in their own country is religious, if not in its intensity, at any rate in its almost absolute and universal authority . . . As children we hear it asserted or implied in the conversation of our elders. Every new stage of our educational training provides some additional testimony on its behalf . . . We may distrust and dislike much that is done in the name of our country by our fellow-country-men; but our country itself, its democratic system, and its prosperous future are above suspicion.[3]

If anybody attributed this sort of civic religion to Americans today, it would be assumed that he was speaking only of the chauvinists—of the Americans who think of John Wayne rather than of Abraham Lincoln as our representative man, and of America as invincible rather than as kind. Novels like Silko's, Stephenson's, Mailer's, and Pynchon's are our equivalent of Adams' resigned pessimism.

It rarely occurs to present-day American leftists to quote either Lincoln or Whitman. It is no longer the case that, in Croly's words, "every new stage of our educational training provides some additional testimony" on behalf of Americans' faith in their country. On the contrary, a contemporary American student may well emerge from college less convinced that her country has a future than when she entered. She may also be less inclined to think that political initiatives can create such a future. The spirit of detached spectatorship, and the inability to think of American citizenship as an opportunity for action, may already have entered such a student's soul.

In this first lecture I shall try to describe the role of Whitman and Dewey in creating the image of America which was ubiquitous on the American Left prior to the Vietnam War. I say "image" rather than "myth" or "ideology" because I do not think that there is a nonmythological, nonideological way of telling a country's story. Calling a story "mythical" or "ideological" would be meaningful only if such stories could be contrasted with an "objective" story. But though objectivity is a useful goal when one is trying to calculate means to ends by predicting the consequences of action, it is of little relevance when one is trying to decide what sort of person or nation to be. Nobody knows what it would be like to try to be objective when attempting to decide what one's country really is, what its history really means, any more than when answering the question of who one really is oneself, what one's individual past really adds up to. We raise questions about our individual or national identity as part of the process of deciding what we will do next, what we will try to become.

As an example of such a process of decision, consider James Baldwin's book *The Fire Next Time.* Early in that book

Baldwin says, "This is the crime of which I accuse my country and my countrymen, and for which neither I nor time nor history will ever forgive them, that they have destroyed and are destroying hundreds of thousands of lives and do not know it and do not want to know it."[4] This lack of forgiveness can easily take the form it does in the theology of the Nation of Islam—with whose prophet, Elijah Muhammad, Baldwin describes an encounter. The Black Muslims say that white people started out as homunculi created by a diabolical scientist. This hypothesis seems to them the best explanation for the inhuman cruelty of the slave auctions and the lynchings.

Those who accept Elijah Muhammad's story use it to convey the wholehearted, gut-wrenching disgust for white America which is manifest in Silko's novel. But as Baldwin's narrative of self-creation unfolds, we watch him combining a continued unwillingness to forgive with a continuing identification with the country that brought over his ancestors in chains. "I am not," he writes, "a ward of America; I am one of the first Americans to arrive on these shores."[5]

In another passage Baldwin says, "In short, we, the black and the white, deeply need each other here if we are really to become a nation—if we are really, that is, to achieve our identity, our maturity, as men and women."[6] He ends his book with a sentence which has been quoted over and over again: "If we—and now I mean the relatively conscious whites and the relatively conscious blacks, who must, like lovers, insist on, or create, the consciousness of the others— do not falter in our duty now, we may be able, handful that we are, to end the racial nightmare, and achieve our country, and change the history of the world." The difference between Elijah Muhammad's decision about how to think of America and the one reached by Baldwin is the difference between deciding to be a spectator and to leave the fate of the United States to the operation of nonhuman forces, and deciding to be an agent.

I do not think there is any point in arguing that Elijah Muhammad made the right decision and Baldwin the wrong one, or vice versa. Neither forgave, but one turned away from the project of achieving the country and the other did not. Both decisions are intelligible. Either can be made plausible. But there are no neutral, objective criteria which dictate one rather than the other.

For the same reasons that I think there is no point in asking whether Baldwin made the right decision, I think there is no point in asking whether Lincoln or Whitman or Dewey got America right. Stories about what a nation has been and should try to be are not attempts at accurate representation, but rather attempts to forge a moral identity. The argument between Left and Right about which episodes in our history we Americans should pride ourselves on will never be a contest between a true and a false account of our country's history and its identity. It is better described as an argument about which hopes to allow ourselves and which to forgo.

As long as our country has a politically active Right and a politically active Left, this argument will continue. It is at the heart of the nation's political life, but the Left is responsible for keeping it going. For the Right never thinks that anything much needs to be changed: it thinks the country is basically in good shape, and may well have been in better shape in the past. It sees the Left's struggle for social justice as mere troublemaking, as utopian foolishness. The Left, by definition, is the party of hope. It insists that our nation remains unachieved. As the historian Nelson Lichtenstein has said, "All of America's great reform movements, from the crusade against slavery to the labor upsurge in the 1930's, defined themselves as champions of a moral and patriotic nationalism, which they counterposed to the parochial and selfish elites which stood athwart their vision of a virtuous society."[7]

Insofar as a Left becomes spectatorial and retrospective, it ceases to be a Left. I shall be claiming in these lectures that the American Left, once the old alliance between the intellectuals and the unions broke down in the course of the Sixties, began to sink into an attitude like Henry Adams'. Leftists in the academy have permitted cultural politics to supplant real politics, and have collaborated with the Right in making cultural issues central to public debate. They are spending energy which should be directed at proposing new laws on discussing topics as remote from the country's needs as were Adams' musings on the Virgin and the Dynamo. The academic Left has no projects to propose to America, no vision of a country to be achieved by building a consensus on the need for specific reforms. Its members no longer feel the force of James's and Croly's rhetoric. The American civic religion seems to them narrow-minded and obsolete nationalism.

Whitman and Dewey were among the prophets of this civic religion. They offered a new account of what America was, in the hope of mobilizing Americans as political agents. The most striking feature of their redescription of our country is its thoroughgoing secularism.[8] In the past, most of the stories that have incited nations to projects of self-improvement have been stories about their obligations to one or more gods. For much of European and American history, nations have asked themselves how they appear in the eyes of the Christian God. American exceptionalism has usually been a belief in special divine favor, as in the writings of Joseph Smith and Billy Graham. By contrast, Elijah Muhammad and Leslie Marmon Silko are examples of inverted exceptionalism: in their visions, white America will be the object of special divine wrath.

Dewey and Whitman wanted Americans to continue to think of themselves as exceptional, but both wanted to drop any reference to divine favor or wrath. They hoped to separate the fraternity and loving kindness urged by the Christian scriptures from the ideas of supernatural parentage, immortality, providence, and—most important—sin. They wanted Americans to take pride in what America might, all by itself and by its own lights, make of itself, rather than in America's obedience to any authority—even the authority of God. Thus Whitman wrote:

> And I call to mankind, Be not curious about God,
> For I who am curious about each am not curious
> about God.[9]

Whitman thought there was no need to be curious about God because there is no standard, not even a divine one, against which the decisions of a free people can be measured. Americans, he hoped, would spend the energy that past human societies had spent on discovering God's desires on discovering one another's desires. Americans will be curious about every other American, but not about anything which claims authority over America.

Kenneth Rexroth claims that Whitman invented the idea of "the realization of the American Dream as an apocalypse, an eschatological event which would give the life of man its ultimate significance." He goes on to say:

> Other religions have been founded on the promise of
> the Community of Love, the Abode of Peace, the King-

dom of God. Whitman identified with his own nation-state. We excuse such ideas only when they began 3,000 years ago in the Levantine desert. In our own time we suspect them of dangerous malevolence. Yet Whitman's vision exposes and explodes all the frauds that pass for the American Way of Life. It is the last and greatest vision of the American potential.[10]

Everything Rexroth says in this passage seems to me correct, except for the phrase "last and greatest." Whitman had successful imitators in his attempt to tie up the history of our nation-state with the meaning of human life. Perhaps because I am a philosophy professor, and have a special interest in philosophical restatements of moral ideals, I think that John Dewey was the most successful and most useful of these imitators.

Whitman explicitly said that he would "use the words America and democracy as convertible terms."[11] Dewey was less explicit, but when he uses "truly democratic" as a supreme honorific, he is obviously envisaging an achieved America. Both Dewey and Whitman viewed the United States as an opportunity to see ultimate significance in a finite, human, historical project, rather than in something eternal and nonhuman. They both hoped that America would be the place where a religion of love would finally replace a religion of fear. They dreamed that Americans would break the traditional link between the religious impulse, the impulse to stand in awe of something greater than oneself, and the infantile need for security, the childish hope of escaping from time and chance. They wanted to preserve the former and discard the latter. They wanted to put hope for a casteless and classless America in the place traditionally occupied by knowledge of the will of God. They wanted that utopian America to replace God as the unconditional object of desire. They wanted the struggle for social justice to be the country's animating principle, the nation's soul.

"Democracy," Dewey said, "is neither a form of government nor a social expediency, but a metaphysic of the relation of man and his experience in nature."[12] For both Whitman and Dewey, the terms "America" and "democracy" are shorthand for a new conception of what it is to be human—a conception which has no room for obedience to a nonhuman authority, and in which nothing save freely achieved consensus among human beings has any authority at all. Steven Rockefeller is right to say that "[Dewey's] goal was to integrate fully the religious life with the American democratic life."[13] But the sort of integration Dewey hoped for is not a matter of blending the worship of an eternal Being with hope for the temporal realization, in America, of this Being's will. It is a matter of forgetting about eternity. More generally, it is a matter of replacing shared knowledge of what is already real with social hope for what might become real.

The word "democracy," Whitman said, "is a great word, whose history . . . remains unwritten, because that history has yet to be enacted."[14]

Forgetting about eternity, and replacing knowledge of the antecedently real with hope for the contingent future, is not easy. But both tasks have been a good deal easier since Hegel. Hegel was the first philosopher to take time and finitude as seriously as any Hobbesian materialist, while at the same time taking the religious impulse as seriously as any Hebrew prophet or Christian saint. Spinoza had attempted such a synthesis by identifying God with Nature, but Spinoza still thought it desirable to see things under the aspect of eternity. Hegel rejoined that any view of human history under that aspect would be too thin and abstract to be of any religious use. He suggested that the meaning of human life is a function of how human history turns out, rather than of the relation of that history to something ahistorical. This suggestion made it easier for two of Hegel's readers, Dewey and Whitman, to claim that the way to think about the significance of the human adventure is to look forward rather than upward: to contrast a possible human future with the human past and present.

Marx, unfortunately, has been the most influential of the left-wing Hegelians. But Marx mistakenly thought that Hegel's dialectic could be used for predictive as well as inspirational purposes. That is why Marxists have produced the form of historicism which Karl Popper rightly criticized as impoverished. But there is another form of Hegelian historicism which survives Popper's criticisms intact. In this form, historicism is simply the temporalization of what Plato, and even Kant, try to eternalize. It is the temporalization of ultimate significance, and of awe.

Dewey's philosophy is a systematic attempt to temporalize everything, to leave nothing fixed. This means abandoning the attempt to find a theoretical frame of reference within which to evaluate proposals for the human future. Dewey's romantic hope was that future events would make every proposed frame obsolete. What he dreaded was stasis: a time in which everybody would take for granted that the purpose of history had been accomplished, an age of spectators rather than agents, a country in which arguments between Right and Left would no longer be heard.

Dewey read a lot of Hegel when he was young. He used Hegel to purge himself first of Kant, and later of orthodox Christianity. Whitman read only a little, but what he read was enough to make him exclaim with delight. "Only Hegel," Whitman wrote in his notebooks, "is fit for America—is large enough and free enough."[15] "I rate [Hegel]," he goes on to say, "as Humanity's chiefest teacher and the choicest loved physician of my mind and soul."[16]

Hegel's philosophy of history legitimized and underwrote Whitman's hope to substitute his own nation-state for the

Kingdom of God. For Hegel told a story about history as the growth of freedom, the gradual dawning of the idea that human beings are on their own, because there is nothing more to God than his march through the world—nothing more to the divine than the history of the human adventure. In a famous passage, Hegel pointed across the Atlantic to a place where as yet unimagined wonders might be worked: "America is the country of the future . . . the land of desire for all those who are weary of the historical arsenal of old Europe."[17]

Whitman probably never encountered this passage, but he knew in his bones that Hegel *should* have written that sentence. It was obvious to him that Hegel had written a prelude to the American saga. Hegel's works, Whitman said, might "not inappropriately be this day collected and bound up under the conspicuous title: *Speculations for the use of North America, and Democracy there.*"[18] This is because Hegel thinks God remains incomplete until he enters time—until, in Christian terminology, he becomes incarnate and suffers on the Cross. Hegel uses the doctrine of Incarnation to turn Greek metaphysics on its head, and to argue that without God the Son, God the Father would remain a mere potentiality, a mere Idea. Without time and suffering, God is, in Hegel's terms, a "mere abstraction." Hegel verges on saying something Whitman actually did say: "The whole theory of the special and supernatural and all that was twined with it or educed out of it departs as a dream . . . It is not consistent with the reality of the soul to admit that there is anything in the universe more divine than men and women."[19]

Whitman, like most American thinkers of the nineteenth century, believed that the Golgotha of the Spirit was in the past, and that the American Declaration of Independence had been an Easter dawn. Because the United States is the first country founded in the hope of a new kind of human fraternity, it would be the place where the promise of the ages would first be realized. Americans would form the vanguard of human history, because, as Whitman says, "the Americans of all nations at any time upon the earth have probably the fullest poetical nature. The United States themselves are essentially the greatest poem."[20] They are also the fulfillment of the human past. "The blossoms we wear in our hats," Whitman wrote, "are the growth of two thousand years."[21]

Whitman thought that we Americans have the most poetical nature because we are the first thoroughgoing experiment in national self-creation: the first nation-state with nobody but itself to please—not even God. We are the greatest poem because we put ourselves in the place of God: our essence is our existence, and our existence is in the future. Other nations thought of themselves as hymns to the glory of God. We redefine God as our future selves.

Neither Dewey nor Whitman, however, was committed to the view that things would *inevitably* go well for America, that the American experiment in self-creation would succeed. The price of temporalization is contingency. Because they rejected any idea of Divine Providence and any idea of immanent teleology, Dewey and Whitman had to grant the possibility that the vanguard of humanity may lose its way, and perhaps lead our species over a cliff. As Whitman put it, "The United States are destined either to surmount the gorgeous history of feudalism, or else prove the most tremendous failure of time."[22] Whereas Marx and Spencer claimed to know what was bound to happen, Whitman and Dewey denied such knowledge in order to make room for pure, joyous hope.

The trouble with Europe, Whitman and Dewey thought, was that it tried too hard for knowledge: it tried to find an answer to the question of what human beings should be like. It hoped to get authoritative guidance for human conduct. One of the first Europeans to suggest abandoning this hope was Wilhelm von Humboldt, a founder of ethnography and a philosopher who greatly influenced Hegel. In a passage which Mill used as the epigraph for his *On Liberty*, von Humboldt wrote that the point of social organization is to make evident "the absolute and essential importance of human development in its richest diversity." Whitman picked up this particular ball from Mill and cited *On Liberty* in the first paragraph of his *Democratic Vistas*. There Whitman says that Mill demands "two main constituents, or sub-strata, for a truly grand nationality—lst, a large variety of character—and 2d, full play for human nature to expand itself in numberless and even conflicting directions."[23]

Mill and Humboldt's "richest diversity" and Whitman's "full play" are ways of saying that no past human achievement, not Plato's or even Christ's, can tell us about the ultimate significance of human life. No such achievement can give us a template on which to model our future. The future will widen endlessly. Experiments with new forms of individual and social life will interact and reinforce one another. Individual life will become unthinkably diverse and social life unthinkably free. The moral we should draw from the European past, and in particular from Christianity, is not instruction about the authority under which we should live, but suggestions about how to make ourselves wonderfully different from anything that has been.

This romance of endless diversity should not, however, be confused with what nowadays is sometimes called "multiculturalism." The latter term suggests a morality of live-and-let-live, a politics of side-by-side development in which members of distinct cultures preserve and protect their own culture against the incursions of other cultures. Whitman, like Hegel, had no interest in preservation or protection. He wanted competition and argument between alternative forms of human life—a poetic agon, in which jarring dialectical discords would be resolved in previously unheard harmonies. The Hegelian idea of "progressive evolution," which was the nineteenth century's great contribution to political and social thought, is that everybody gets played off against everybody else. This should occur nonviolently if possible, but violently if necessary, as was in fact necessary in America in 1861. The Hegelian hope is that the result of such struggles will be a new culture, better than any of those of which it is the synthesis.[24] This new culture will be better because it will contain more variety in unity—it will be a tapestry in which more strands have been woven together. But this tapestry, too, will eventually have to be torn to shreds in order that a larger one may be woven, in order that the past may not obstruct the future.

There is, I think, little difference in doctrine between Dewey and Whitman. But there is an obvious difference in emphasis: the difference between talking mostly about love and talking mostly about citizenship. Whitman's image of democracy was of lovers embracing. Dewey's was of a town meeting. Dewey dwelt on the need to create what the Israeli philosopher Avishai Margalit has called a *decent* society, defined as one in which *institutions* do not humiliate. Whitman's hopes were centered on the creation of what Margalit calls, by contrast, a *civilized* society, defined as one in which *individuals* do not humiliate each other—in which tolerance for other people's fantasies and choices is instinctive and habitual.[25] Dewey's principal target was institutionalized selfishness, whereas Whitman's was the socially acceptable sadism which is a consequence of sexual repression, and of the inability to love.

Dewey disliked and distrusted Franklin D. Roosevelt, but many of his ideas came into their own in the New Deal. Whitman's hopes, on the other hand, began to be realized only in the youth culture of the 1960s. Whitman would have been delighted by rock-and-roll, drugs, and the kind of casual, friendly copulation which is insouciant about the homosexual-heterosexual distinction. The historiography of the Sixties has come to be dominated by New Left politics, but we need to remember that lots of young people in the Sixties viewed Tom Hayden with the same suspicion as they viewed Lyndon Johnson. Their principal concern was cultural rather than political change.[26] Dewey might have approved of the rock-and-roll culture in a guarded and deliberate way, but Whitman would have thrown himself into it wholeheartedly.[27]

Dewey would not have expressed his desire to exalt and encourage his country by saying, as Whitman did, that he "who would be the greatest poet" must "attract his own land body and soul to himself and hang on its neck with incomparable love and plunge his seminal muscle into its merits and demerits."[28] But Dewey might have written other bits of *Leaves of Grass*—for example, "I speak the password primeval . . . I give the sign of democracy;/By God! I will accept nothing which all cannot have their counterpart of on the same terms."[29] One can also imagine him writing:

> Logic and sermons never convince,
> The damp of night drives deeper into my soul.

> Only what proves itself to every man and woman
>   is so,
> Only what nobody denies is so.[30]

These passages in Whitman can be read as presaging the doctrine that made pragmatism both original and infamous: its refusal to believe in the existence of Truth, in the sense of something not made by human hands, something which has authority over human beings. The closest Hegel got to this pragmatist doctrine was his dictum that philosophy is its own time held in thought.

Despite this historicism, Hegel could never bring himself to assert the primacy of the practical over the theoretical—what Hilary Putnam, defining the essence of pragmatism, has called the primacy of the agent point of view. Dewey, like Marx in the Eleventh Thesis on Feuerbach, took the primacy of the practical all the way. His pragmatism is an answer to the question "What can philosophy do for the United States?" rather than to the question "How can the United States be philosophically justified?" He abandoned the question "Why should one prefer democracy to feudalism, and self-creation to obedience to authority?" in favor of the question "Given the preferences we Americans share, given the adventure on which we are embarked, what should we say about truth, knowledge, reason, virtue, human nature, and all the other traditional philosophical topics?" America will, Dewey hoped, be the first nation-state to have the courage to renounce hope of justification from on high—from a source which is immovable and eternal. Such a country will treat both its philosophy and its poetry as modes of self-expression, rather than ask its philosophers to provide it with reassurance.

The culminating achievement of Dewey's philosophy was to treat evaluative terms such as "true" and "right" not as signifying a relation to some antecedently existing thing—such as God's Will, or Moral Law, or the Intrinsic Nature of Objective Reality—but as expressions of satisfaction at having found a solution to a problem: a problem which may someday seem obsolete, and a satisfaction which may someday seem misplaced. The effect of this treatment is to change our account of progress. Instead of seeing progress as a matter of getting closer to something specifiable in advance, we see it as a matter of solving more problems. Progress is, as Thomas Kuhn suggested, measured by the extent to which we have made ourselves better than we were in the past rather than by our increased proximity to a goal.

Late in his life, Dewey tried to "state briefly the democratic faith in the formal terms of a philosophical proposition." The proposition was that democracy is the only form of moral and social faith which does not "rest upon the idea that experience must be subjected at some point or other to some form of external control: to some 'authority' alleged to exist outside the processes of experience."[31] This formulation echoes Whitman's exclamation, "How long it takes to make this American world see that it is, in itself, the final authority and reliance!"[32] Antiauthoritarianism is the motive behind Dewey's opposition to Platonic and theocentric metaphysics, and behind his more original and far more controversial opposition to the correspondence theory of truth: the idea that truth is a matter of accurate representation of an antecedently existing reality. For Dewey, the idea that there was a reality "out there" with an intrinsic nature to be respected and corresponded to was not a manifestation of sound common sense. It was a relic of Platonic otherworldliness.

Repudiating the correspondence theory of truth was Dewey's way of restating, in philosophical terms, Whitman's claim that America does not need to place itself within a frame of reference. Great Romantic poems, such as "Song of Myself" or the United States of America, are supposed to break through previous frames of reference, not be intelligible within them. To say that the United States themselves are essentially the greatest poem is to say that America will create the taste by which it will be judged. It is to envisage our nation-state as both self-creating poet and self-created poem.

So much for my interpretation of Whitman's and Dewey's attempts thoroughly to secularize America—to see America as the paradigmatic democracy, and thus as the country which would pride itself as one in which governments and social institutions exist only for the purpose of making a new sort of individual possible, one who will take nothing as authoritative save free consensus between as diverse a variety of citizens as can possibly be produced. Such a country cannot contain castes or classes, because the kind of self-respect which is needed for free participation in democratic deliberation is incompatible with such social divisions.

For Whitman and Dewey, a classless and casteless society—the sort of society which American leftists have spent the twentieth century trying to construct—is neither more natural nor more rational than the cruel societies of feudal Europe or of eighteenth-century Virginia. All that can be said in its defense is that it would produce less unnecessary suffering than any other, and that it is the best means to a certain end: the creation of a greater diversity of individuals—larger, fuller, more imaginative and daring individuals. To those who want a demonstration that less suffering and greater diversity should be the overriding aims of political endeavor, Dewey and Whitman have nothing to say. They know of no more certain premises from which such a belief might be deduced.

This conception of the purpose of social organization is a specifically leftist one. The Left, the party of hope, sees our country's moral identity as still to be achieved, rather than as needing to be preserved. The Right thinks that our country already has a moral identity, and hopes to keep that identity intact. It fears economic and political change, and therefore easily becomes the pawn of the rich and powerful—the people whose selfish interests are served by forestalling such change.

I do not think that subsequent American leftists have made any advance on Dewey's understanding of the relation between the individual and society. Dewey was as convinced as Foucault that the subject is a social construction, that discursive practices go all the way down to the bottom of our minds and hearts. But he insisted that the only point of society is to construct subjects capable of ever more novel, ever richer, forms of human happiness. The vocabulary in which Dewey suggested we discuss our social problems and our political initiatives was part of his attempt to develop a discursive practice suitable for that project of social construction.

To take pride in collaborating in this project is not to endorse what Baldwin called the

collection of myths to which white Americans cling: that their ancestors were all freedom-loving heroes, that they were born in the greatest country the world has ever seen, or that Americans are invincible in battle and wise in peace, that Americans have always dealt honorably with Mexicans and Indians and all other neighbors or inferiors, that American men are the world's most direct and virile, that American women are pure.[33]

The sort of pride Whitman and Dewey urged Americans to feel is compatible with remembering that we expanded our boundaries by massacring the tribes which blocked our way, that we broke the word we had pledged in the Treaty of Guadalupe Hidalgo, and that we caused the death of a million Vietnamese out of sheer macho arrogance.

But, one might protest, is there then *nothing* incompatible with American national pride? I think the Dewey-Whitman answer is that there are many things that should chasten and temper such pride, but that nothing a nation has done should make it impossible for a constitutional democracy to regain self-respect. To say that certain acts *do* make this impossible is to abandon the secular, antiauthoritarian vocabulary of shared social hope in favor of the vocabulary which Whitman and Dewey abhorred: a vocabulary built around the notion of sin.

People who take this latter notion seriously find Dewey and Whitman childlike, naive, and dangerous. They see both as lacking a sense of the tragic, of the abyss. For such people, it is a fundamental moral fact that the commission of certain acts—acts which can be specified without regard for historical changes or cultural differences—is incompatible with further self-respect. But Dewey has a different conception of the fundamental moral fact. For him what makes us moral beings is that, for each of us, there are some acts we believe we ought to die rather than commit. Which acts these are will differ from epoch to epoch, and from person to person, but to be a moral agent is to be unable to imagine living with oneself after committing these acts.

But now suppose that one has in fact done one of the things one could not have imagined doing, and finds that one is still alive. At that point, one's choices are suicide, a life of bottomless self-disgust, and an attempt to live so as never to do such a thing again. Dewey recommends the third choice. He thinks you should remain an agent, rather than either committing suicide or becoming a horrified spectator of your own past. He regards self-loathing as a luxury which agents—either individuals or nations—cannot afford. He was quite aware of the possibility, and indeed the likelihood, of tragedy.[34] But he utterly repudiated the idea of sin as an explanation of tragedy.

People who take the notion of sin seriously—admirers of Saint Augustine such as Reinhold Niebuhr and Jean Bethke Elshtain—are appalled by this line of thought.[35] They view it as merely the light-minded, Californian view that one should treat any crime one happens to commit as a useful learning experience. But Andrew Delbanco gets Dewey exactly right when he says that for him "evil was the failure of imagina-

tion to reach beyond itself, the human failure to open oneself
to a spirit that both chastises one for confidence in one's own
righteousness and promises the enduring comfort of recip-
rocal love. There is a sense in which all of Dewey's thought
was an extended commentary on Emerson's remark 'the only
sin is limitation.'" Delbanco goes on to say, correctly, that
this understanding of evil was basic to the Progressive Movement in American politics, and to its confidence in education
and social reform. He is also correct when he concludes that
"such a view of the human imagination as restless within established forms had no room for the idea of a fixed standard
by which deviance from the truth could be measured and denounced."[36]

Delbanco has his doubts about whether we can afford to
abandon the idea of such a standard. Leo Strauss, Harvey
Mansfield, and many others have no such doubts. They see
belief in such a standard as essential to individual and social
decency. But what these critics see as Dewey's naiveté and
light-mindedness I see as his intellectual courage—the
courage to abandon the idea that it is possible to attain, in either science or morals, what Hilary Putnam calls a "God's-
eye view." Dewey abandoned the idea that one can say how
things really are, as opposed to how they might best be described in order to meet some particular human need. In this
respect he is in agreement with Nietzsche, and with such
critics of "the metaphysics of presence" as Derrida and Hei-

degger. For all these philosophers, objectivity is a matter of intersubjective consensus among human beings, not of accurate representation of something nonhuman. Insofar as human beings do not share the same needs, they may disagree about what is objectively the case. But the resolution of such disagreement cannot be an appeal to the way reality, apart from any human need, really is. The resolution can only be political: one must use democratic institutions and procedures to conciliate these various needs, and thereby widen the range of consensus about how things are.

Those who find this line of philosophical thought horrifying do not agree with Dewey and Foucault that the subject is a social construction, and that discursive practices go all the way down. They think that moral idealism depends on moral universalism—on an appeal to universally shared demands, built into human nature, or to the nature of social practice. I have argued against this claim in the past, and I shall not use these lectures to do so again. Instead, I shall end by returning to the contrast between agents and spectators with which I began.

I said earlier that we now have, among many American students and teachers, a spectatorial, disgusted, mocking Left rather than a Left which dreams of achieving our country. This is not the only Left we have, but it is the most prominent and vocal one. Members of this Left find America unforgivable, as Baldwin did, and also unachievable, as he did not.

This leads them to step back from their country and, as they say, "theorize" it. It leads them to do what Henry Adams did: to give cultural politics preference over real politics, and to mock the very idea that democratic institutions might once again be made to serve social justice. It leads them to prefer knowledge to hope.

I see this preference as a turn away from secularism and pragmatism—as an attempt to do precisely what Dewey and Whitman thought should not be done: namely, to see the American adventure within a fixed frame of reference, a frame supplied by theory. Paradoxically, the leftists who are most concerned not to "totalize," and who insist that everything be seen as the play of discursive differences rather than in the old metaphysics-of-presence way, are also the most eager to theorize, to become spectators rather than agents.[37] But that is helping yourself with one hand to what you push away with the other. The further you get from Greek metaphysics, Dewey urged, the less anxious you should be to find a frame within which to fit an ongoing historical process.

This retreat from secularism and pragmatism to theory has accompanied a revival of ineffability. We are told over and over again that Lacan has shown human desire to be inherently unsatisfiable, that Derrida has shown meaning to be undecidable, that Lyotard has shown commensuration between oppressed and oppressors to be impossible, and that events such as the Holocaust or the massacre of the original Americans are unrepresentable. Hopelessness has become fashionable on the Left—principled, theorized, philosophical hopelessness. The Whitmanesque hope which lifted the hearts of the American Left before the 1960s is now thought to have been a symptom of a naive "humanism."

I see this preference for knowledge over hope as repeating the move made by leftist intellectuals who, earlier in the century, got their Hegelianism from Marx rather than Dewey. Marx thought we should be scientific rather than merely utopian—that we should interpret the historical events of our day within a larger theory. Dewey did not. He thought one had to view these events as the protocols of social experiments whose outcomes are unpredictable.

The Foucauldian Left represents an unfortunate regression to the Marxist obsession with scientific rigor. This Left still wants to put historical events in a theoretical context. It exaggerates the importance of philosophy for politics, and wastes its energy on sophisticated theoretical analyses of the significance of current events. But Foucauldian theoretical sophistication is even more useless to leftist politics than was Engels' dialectical materialism. Engels at least had an eschatology. Foucauldians do not even have that. Because they regard liberal reformist initiatives as symptoms of a discredited liberal "humanism," they have little interest in designing new social experiments.

This distrust of humanism, with its retreat from practice to theory, is the sort of failure of nerve which leads people to abandon secularism for a belief in sin, and in Delbanco's "fixed standard by which deviance from the truth can be measured and denounced." It leads them to look for a frame of reference outside the process of experimentation and decision that is an individual or a national life. Grand theories— eschatologies like Hegel's or Marx's, inverted eschatologies like Heidegger's, and rationalizations of hopelessness like Foucault's and Lacan's—satisfy the urges that theology used to satisfy. These are urges which Dewey hoped Americans might cease to feel. Dewey wanted Americans to share a civic religion that substituted utopian striving for claims to theological knowledge.

In the remaining lectures I shall be contrasting the Deweyan, pragmatic, participatory Left as it existed prior to the Vietnam War and the spectatorial Left which has taken its place. One consequence of that disastrous war was a generation of Americans who suspected that our country was unachievable—that that war not only could never be forgiven, but had shown us to be a nation conceived in sin, and irredeemable. This suspicion lingers. As long as it does, and as long as the American Left remains incapable of national pride, our country will have only a cultural Left, not a political one.

THE ECLIPSE

OF THE

REFORMIST

LEFT

It is impossible to discuss leftist politics in the twentieth century, in any country, without saying something about Marxism. For Marxism was not only a catastrophe for all the countries in which Marxists took power, but a disaster for the reformist Left in all the countries in which they did not.

At the end of the twentieth century, Marxism is in the position of Roman Catholicism at the end of the seventeenth. By then the full horror of the Renaissance papacies and of the Inquisition had been made known. Many Christians thought that it would be best for the bishops of Rome to close up shop. Christianity, they pointed out, had long antedated the papacy, and would be much better off for its demise.

Many present-day eastern and central Europeans hold an analogous view about Marxism, and I think they are right. The ideals of social democracy and economic justice, these people say, long antedated Marxism, and would have made much more headway had "Marxism-Leninism" never been invented. Now that the last general secretary of the Communist Party of the USSR has pointed out how much better off Russia would have been if Lenin had failed, people on the Left should stop being sentimental about the Bolshevik Revolution.[1] Leftists should repudiate links with Lenin as firmly as the early Protestants repudiated the doctrine of the Primacy of Peter.

For us Americans, it is important not to let Marxism influence the story we tell about our own Left. We should repudi-

ate the Marxists' insinuation that only those who are convinced capitalism must be overthrown can count as leftists,
and that everybody else is a wimpy liberal, a self-deceiving
bourgeois reformer.[2] Many recent histories of the Sixties
have, unfortunately, been influenced by Marxism. These histories distinguish the emergent student Left and the so-called
Old Left from the "liberals"—a term used to cover both the
people who administered the New Deal and those whom
Kennedy brought from Harvard to the White House in 1961.

In such histories, you are counted as a member of the Old
Left only if you had proclaimed yourself a socialist early on,
and if you continued to express grave doubts about the via-
bility of capitalism.[3] So, in the historiography which has unfortunately become standard, Irving Howe and Michael Harrington count as leftists, but John Kenneth Galbraith and
Arthur Schlesinger do not, even though these four men pro-
moted mostly the same causes and thought about our country's problems in pretty much the same terms.

I think we should abandon the leftist-versus-liberal distinction, along with the other residues of Marxism that clut-
ter up our vocabulary—overworked words like "commod-
ification" and "ideology," for example. Had Kerensky
managed to ship Lenin back to Zurich, Marx would still have
been honored as a brilliant political economist who foresaw
how the rich would use industrialization to immiserate the
poor. But his philosophy of history would have seemed, like

Herbert Spencer's, a nineteenth-century curiosity. People on the Left would not have wasted their time on Marxist scholasticism, nor would they have been so ready to assume that the nationalization of the means of production was the only way to achieve social justice. They would have evaluated suggestions for preventing the immiseration of the proletariat country by country, in the pragmatic, experimental spirit which Dewey recommended. The contrast between genuine revolutionary leftists and wishy-washy liberal reformers would never have taken hold.

I think we should drop the term "Old Left" as a name for the Americans who called themselves "socialists" between 1945 and 1964. I propose to use the term "reformist Left" to cover all those Americans who, between 1900 and 1964, struggled within the framework of constitutional democracy to protect the weak from the strong. This includes lots of people who called themselves "communists" and "socialists," and lots of people who never dreamed of calling themselves either. I shall use "New Left" to mean the people—mostly students—who decided, around 1964, that it was no longer possible to work for social justice within the system.

In my sense of the term, Woodrow Wilson—the president who kept Eugene Debs in jail but appointed Louis Brandeis to the Supreme Court—counts as a part-time leftist. So does FDR—the president who created the rudiments of a welfare state and urged workers to join labor unions, while obdurately turning his back on African-Americans. So does Lyndon Johnson, who permitted the slaughter of hundreds of thousands of Vietnamese children, but also did more for poor children in the United States than any previous president. I cannot offer, and we do not need, a criterion specifying how much time a politician must spend on leftist reforms to be counted as a man or woman of the Left. My term "reformist Left" is intended to cover most of the people who were feared and hated by the Right, and thereby to smudge the line which the Marxists tried to draw between leftists and liberals.

Erasing that line is easier if we reflect that the Communist Party of the United States was of very little importance to the political life of our country. It marshaled some good picket lines, and it recruited a few good agents for Soviet intelligence. But the most enduring effects of its activities were the careers of men like Martin Dies, Richard Nixon, and Joseph McCarthy. On the other hand, we should remember that individual members of that party worked heroically, and made very painful sacrifices, in the hope of helping our country to achieve its promise. Many Marxists, even those who spent decades apologizing for Stalin, helped change our country for the better by helping to change its laws. So did many managerial technocrats in the Kennedy White House, even those who later helped Johnson wage the Vietnam War.

It would be a good idea to stop asking when it was unforgivably late, or unforgivably early, to have left the Commu-

nist Party. We should also stop asking when it was too late, or
too early, to have come out against the Vietnam War. A hundred years from now, Howe and Galbraith, Harrington and
Schlesinger, Wilson and Debs, Jane Addams and Angela
Davis, Felix Frankfurter and John L. Lewis, W. E. B. Du Bois
and Eleanor Roosevelt, Robert Reich and Jesse Jackson, will
all be remembered for having advanced the cause of social
justice. They will all be seen as having been "on the Left."
The difference between these people and men like Calvin
Coolidge, Irving Babbitt, T. S. Eliot, Robert Taft, and William
Buckley will be far clearer than any of the quarrels which
once divided them among themselves. Whatever mistakes
they made, these people will deserve, as Coolidge and Buckley never will, the praise with which Jonathan Swift ended
his own epitaph: "Imitate him if you can; he served human
liberty."

If we look for people who made no mistakes, who were always on the right side, who never apologized for tyrants or
unjust wars, we shall have few heroes and heroines. Marxism
encouraged us to look for such purity. Marxists suggested
that only the revolutionary proletariat could embody virtue,
that bourgeois reformers were "objectively reactionary,"
and that failure to take Marx's scenario seriously was proof of
complicity with the forces of darkness. Marxism was, as Paul
Tillich and others rightly noted, more of a religion than a
secularist program for social change. Like all fundamental-

ist sects, it emphasized purity. Lenin, like Savonarola, demanded complete freedom from sin and undeviating obedience.

Some socially useful thinkers—for example, Cornel West, Fredric Jameson, and Terry Eagleton—still speak of themselves, for what seem to me purely sentimental reasons, as "Marxists." Such sentimentality appalls Poles and Hungarians who never want to hear Marx's name again. I suspect it would baffle the Chinese dissidents starving in the laogai. Nevertheless, there is little harm in such nostalgic piety. For in the mouths of these people the word "Marxism" signals hardly more than an awareness that the rich are still ripping off the poor, bribing the politicians, and having almost everything their own way.

One way to convince oneself that the American Left could have gotten along perfectly well without Marxism is to look back to the best-known manifesto of the Progressive Era, Herbert Croly's *The Promise of American Life*. This book is filled with the same national pride that filled *Democratic Vistas*, but Croly makes a distinction Whitman rarely made: that between America before and America after the coming of industrial capitalism. Whitman was the first Romantic poet to celebrate an industrial and technological civilization, but he did not worry about the phenomenon that Marx and Croly recognized: the immiseration that would occur whenever the capitalists became able to maintain a reserve army of unemployed, and thus to pay starvation wages to those they hire. In late nineteenth- and early twentieth-century America, this reserve army was drawn from the endless supply of European immigrants—the people whose working and living conditions Upton Sinclair described in *The Jungle*, published three years before Croly's book.

Croly begins his book by saying that Americans are entitled to their "almost religious faith" in their country. But then he gets down to the problem which the Progressives wanted to solve, the problem created by the fact that "the traditional American confidence in individual freedom has resulted in a morally and socially undesirable distribution of wealth."[4] This new distribution of wealth, Croly realized, threatened to make nonsense of Hegel's suggestion that America might become something gloriously different from Europe, and of Whitman's hope that Lincoln's heirs would see an unending series of new births of human freedom. "So long as the great majority of the poor in any country are inert and are laboring without any hope in this world," Croly wrote, "the whole associated life of that community rests on an equivocal foundation. Its moral and social order is tied to an economic system which starves and mutilates the great majority of the population, and under such conditions its religion necessarily becomes a spiritual drug, administered for the purpose of subduing the popular discontent and relieving the popular misery."[5]

Croly, like Dewey, urged people to set aside the individualist rhetoric of nineteenth-century America. That rhetoric has been the mainstay of the American Right throughout our century, and is now, bafflingly, being treated as characteristic of liberalism by the so-called communitarians. But neither Croly nor Dewey, nor the leaders of the trade union movement, had any use for what the communitarians call "liberal individualism." Croly wrote that "a more highly socialized democracy is the only practicable substitute on the part of convinced democrats for an excessively individualized democracy."[6] It is time, he believed, to set about developing what he called "a dominant and constructive national purpose." In becoming "responsible for the subordination of the individual to that purpose," he said, "the American state will in effect be making itself responsible for a morally and socially desirable distribution of wealth."[7] From 1909 until the present, the thesis that the state must make itself responsible for such redistribution has marked the dividing line between the American Left and the American Right. We Americans did not need Marx to show us the need for redistribution, or to tell us that the state was often little more than the executive committee of the rich and powerful.

To the many readers who found Croly convincing, American nationalism became indistinguishable from what they sometimes called "Christian socialism" and sometimes simply "socialism"—their name for the attempt to create a cooperative commonwealth, a classless society in which nobody should be deprived of his or her dignity as an American citizen by "laboring without any hope of reward in this world." As Croly put it, "In this country, the solution of the social problem demands the substitution of a conscious social ideal for the earlier instinctive homogeneity of the American nation."[8]

Many Progressives who never dreamed of fomenting a revolution or urging the nationalization of the means of production were happy to call themselves "socialists." Twenty years before Croly, the great Wisconsin economist Richard Ely had identified the "New Nationalism" with "the American type of socialism," and had asked his audience to realize that "from every land the wage-earning classes are looking to America for inspiration and direction."[9] Ely's book *Social Aspects of Christianity* argued that industrial capitalism had produced "the farthest and deepest reaching crisis known to human history."[10] He hoped that American intellectuals would throw themselves into the struggle to give the masses what they wanted and deserved.

Eldon Eisenach has argued persuasively that Croly's manifesto of 1909 summarizes two decades' worth of what we should nowadays call "communitarian" criticisms of American individualism—criticisms made by social scientists like Ely and social workers like Jane Addams. These criticisms produced what Eisenach calls a redefinition of American

identity "in nationalist and historicist terms," thereby de-
valuing "prevailing constitutionalist, legalistic and party-
electoral expressions of citizenship."[11] These criticisms
helped substitute a rhetoric of fraternity and national solidarity for a rhetoric of individual rights, and this new rhetoric
was ubiquitous on the Left until the 1960s.

Eisenach has also shown how Progressive intellectuals
turned American universities into what he calls "something
like a national 'church'—the main repository and protector
of common American values, common American meanings,
and common American identities."[12] This new church
preached that America could be true to itself only if it turned
left—that socialism, in some form or another, was necessary
if our country, its government, and its press were not to be
bought up by the rich and greedy. The ministers of this national church told America that it would lose its soul if it did
not devote itself to "a conscious social ideal."

The period in which the state universities of the Midwest
emerged as power bases for redistributivist social initiatives
was also the era of the first great strikes. These strikes were
examples of the kind of solidarity, and of comradeship in
suffering, which Americans had previously witnessed only
in wartime. Now Americans were making sacrifices, and
sometimes dying, not to preserve the republic from political
division, but to preserve it from dividing into a nation of rich
and a nation of poor.

I can sum up by saying that it would be a good thing if the next generation of American leftists found as little resonance in the names of Karl Marx and Vladimir Ilyich Lenin as in those of Herbert Spencer and Benito Mussolini. It would be an even better thing if the names of Ely and Croly, Dreiser and Debs, A. Philip Randolph and John L. Lewis were more familiar to these leftists than they were to the students of the Sixties. For it would be a big help to American efforts for social justice if each new generation were able to think of itself as participating in a movement which has lasted for more than a century, and has served human liberty well. It would help if students became as familiar with the Pullman Strike, the Great Coalfield War,[13] and the passage of the Wagner Act as with the march from Selma, the Berkeley free-speech demonstrations, and Stonewall. Each new generation of students ought to think of American leftism as having a long and glorious history. They should be able to see, as Whitman and Dewey did, the struggle for social justice as central to their country's moral identity.

To bring this about, it would help if American leftists stopped asking whether or not Walter Reuther's attempt to bourgeoisify the auto workers was objectively reactionary. It would also help if they emphasized the similarities rather than the differences between Malcolm X and Bayard Rustin, between Susan B. Anthony and Emma Goldman, between Catharine MacKinnon and Judith Butler. The sectarian divisions which plagued Marxism are manifestations of an urge for purity which the Left would be better off without.

America is not a morally pure country. No country ever has been or ever will be. Nor will any country ever have a morally pure, homogeneous Left. In democratic countries you get things done by compromising your principles in order to form alliances with groups about whom you have grave doubts. The Left in America has made a lot of progress by doing just that. The closest the Left ever came to taking over the government was in 1912, when a Whitman enthusiast, Eugene Debs, ran for president and got almost a million votes. These votes were cast by, as Daniel Bell puts it, "as unstable a compound as was ever mixed in the modern history of political chemistry." This compound mingled rage at low wages and miserable working conditions with, as Bell says, "the puritan conscience of millionaire socialists, the boyish romanticism of a Jack London, the pale Christian piety of a George Herron, . . . the reckless braggadocio of a 'Wild Bill' Haywood, . . . the tepid social-work impulse of do-gooders, . . . the flaming discontent of the dispossessed farmers, the inarticulate and amorphous desire to 'belong' of the immigrant workers, the iconoclastic idol-breaking of the literary radicals, . . . and more."[14]

Those dispossessed farmers were often racist, nativist, and sadistic. The millionaire socialists, ruthless robber barons though they were, nevertheless set up the foundations which sponsored the research which helped get leftist legislation passed. We need to get rid of the Marxist idea that only bottom-up initiatives, conducted by workers and peasants who have somehow been so freed from resentment as to show no trace of prejudice, can achieve our country. The history of leftist politics in America is a story of how top-down initiatives and bottom-up initiatives have interlocked.

Top-down leftist initiatives come from people who have enough security, money, and power themselves, but nevertheless worry about the fate of people who have less. Examples of such initiatives are muckraking exposés by journalists, novelists, and scholars—for example, Ida Tarbell on Standard Oil, Upton Sinclair on immigrant workers in the Chicago slaughterhouses, Noam Chomsky on the State Department's lies and the *New York Times*'s omissions. Other examples are the Wagner and Norris-Laguardia Acts, novels of social protest like *People of the Abyss* and *Studs Lonigan*, the closing of university campuses after the American invasion of Cambodia, and the Supreme Court's decisions in *Brown v. Board of Education* and *Romer v. Evans*.

Bottom-up leftist initiatives come from people who have little security, money, or power and who rebel against the unfair treatment which they, or others like them, are receiving. Examples are the Pullman Strike, Marcus Garvey's black nationalist movement, the General Motors sit-down strike of 1936, the Montgomery bus boycott, the creation of the Mississippi Freedom Democratic Party, the creation of Cesar Chavez's United Farm Workers, and the Stonewall "riot" (the beginning of the gay rights movement).

Although these two kinds of initiatives reinforced each other, the people at the bottom took the risks, suffered the beatings, made all the big sacrifices, and were sometimes murdered. But their heroism might have been fruitless if leisured, educated, relatively risk-free people had not joined the struggle. Those beaten to death by the goon squads and the lynch mobs might have died in vain if the safe and secure had not lent a hand.

These loans were unheroic but indispensable. The Luce journalists of 1937 who filled the pages of *Life* magazine with pictures of the National Guard beating up striking United Automobile Workers were not taking many risks.[15] Nor were the TV reporters who kept the cameras focused on Bull Connor's dogs and cattle prods in 1961. But if they had not been there, and if a lot of secure and well-off Americans had not reacted to those images as they did, the UAW strike against Ford and the Freedom Ride through Alabama would both have been ineffectual. Somebody has to convince the voters that what the authorities are calling senseless violence is actually heroic civil disobedience.

The conviction that the vast inequalities within American society could be corrected by using the institutions of a constitutional democracy—that a cooperative commonwealth

could be created by electing the right politicians and passing
the right laws—held the non-Marxist American Left together
from Croly's time until the early 1960s. But the Vietnam War
splintered that Left. Todd Gitlin believes August 1964 marks
the break in the leftist students' sense of what their country
was like. That was the month in which the Mississippi Freedom Democratic Party was denied seats at the Democratic
Convention in Atlantic City, and in which Congress passed
the Tonkin Gulf Resolution.

Gitlin argues plausibly that these two events "fatefully
turned the movement"[16] and "drew a sharp line through the
New Left's Sixties."[17] Before them, most of the New Left's
rhetoric was consensual and reformist. After them, it began
to build up to the full-throated calls for revolution with
which the decade ended. Whether or not one agrees with
Gitlin about the exact date, it is certainly the case that the
mid-Sixties saw the beginning of the end of a tradition of
leftist reformism which dated back to the Progressive Era.[18]
For reasons I shall be saying more about in my final lecture,
this tradition was never fully reconstituted after the Sixties
came to a close.

Those who admire the revolutionary turn which the New
Left took in the late Sixties have offered us their own accounts
of the history of the American Left. Much of the tone and emphasis of these accounts comes from the writings of C. Wright
Mills and Christopher Lasch. I think the description of mid-

century America which these two men helped put in circulation needs to be replaced. It should be replaced with a story which gives the reformers their due, and thereby leaves more room for national pride and national hope. Emphasizing the continuity between Herbert Croly and Lyndon Johnson, between John Dewey and Martin Luther King, between Eugene Debs and Walter Reuther, would help us to recall a reformist Left which deserves not only respect but imitation—the best model available for the American Left in the coming century. If the intellectuals and the unions could ever get back together again, and could reconstitute the kind of Left which existed in the Forties and Fifties, the first decade of the twenty-first century might conceivably be a Second Progressive Era.

Here is a rough sketch of the argument which convinced Mills, Lasch, and many young leftists of the Sixties to break with the old, reformist Left: The Vietnam War, they rightly said, is an atrocity of which Americans should be deeply ashamed. But, they continued, the Vietnam War is just the latest phase of the anticommunist Cold War. Most of the people in the universities, the unions, and the Democratic Party who call themselves either "liberals" or "leftists" are anticommunists; so we who oppose the war must form a Left which is not anticommunist.

Any attempt to replace the Mills-Lasch account of the history of the post–World War II Left must begin by asking: Granted that the Vietnam War was an atrocity of which America must always be ashamed, does this mean that the Cold War should not have been fought? This question will be debated as long as members of my generation of leftists survive. Those of us who were, like myself, militantly anticommunist believe that the war against Stalin was as legitimate, and as needed, as the war against Hitler. Some of my contemporaries, like Fredric Jameson, still agree with Jean-Paul Sartre. Sartre said that he had always believed, and would always believe, that anticommunists are scum. Such people see the Cold War as nothing more than an American drive for world domination. They mock the idea that America could have prosecuted that war without propping up right-wing dictators. My anticommunist side of the argument gets a lot of support from leftists in central and eastern Europe. Jameson's side of the argument gets a lot of support among leftists in Latin America and Asia—people who have first-hand knowledge of what the CIA can do to a poor nation's hopes for social justice.[19]

People on my side of the argument never took seriously C. Wright Mills's suggestion that American intellectuals should have refused to fight the Cold War, and should have "attempted to get in touch with [their] opposite numbers in all countries, above all in the Sino-Soviet zone . . . [and] make our own separate peace."[20] Our Russian and Polish opposite numbers did not want a separate peace. They wanted liberation from a thuggish, cruel, and seemingly invincible tyranny. Unless America had fought the Cold War, they now believe, they would never have been freed. People on my side of the argument think these Russians and Poles are right. Despite the suggestions of revisionist historians of the Cold War, we do not believe the liberation of 1989 would ever have occurred if the United States had come to terms with Stalin in the late 1940s in the way these historians have suggested was possible. We think that history will see the Cold War as having been fought, like most wars, from thoroughly mixed motives, but as having saved the world from a great danger.

My leftmost students, who are also my favorite students, find it difficult to take my anticommunism seriously. When I tell them that I was a teenage Cold War liberal, they react as they would to the title of a particularly tasteless horror film. So I try to explain to them what it was like to be what Gitlin calls a "red-diaper anticommunist baby." There were lots of babies like me in the Thirties and Forties, but Gitlin's term puzzles his younger readers. I shall spend a few minutes on autobiography in the hope of giving you a sense both of what it was like to grow up on the anticommunist reformist Left in mid-century, and of the continuity between that Left and the Left of 1910, the time of Debs and Croly.

My parents were loyal fellow-travelers of the Communist Party up through 1932, the year after I was born. In that year my father ran a front organization called the League of Professional Groups for Foster and Ford (the Communist Party's candidates for president and vice-president). My parents broke with the party after realizing the extent to which it was run from Moscow, and so I did not get to read the *Daily Worker* when I was a boy. By 1935 the *Worker* was printing cartoons of my father as a trained seal, catching fish thrown by William Randolph Hearst. But my parents did subscribe to the organ of Norman Thomas' Socialist Party, *The Call*, as well as to those of the DeLeonite Socialist Labor Party and the Shachtmanite Socialist Workers' Party. I plowed through these papers, convinced that doing so would teach me how to think about my country and its politics.

Few of the people who wrote for leftist periodicals, either those aimed at workers or those aimed at bourgeois intellectuals like my parents, had any doubt that America was a great, noble, progressive country in which justice would eventually triumph. By "justice" they all meant pretty much the same thing—decent wages and working conditions, and the end of racial prejudice.

They sometimes quoted my maternal grandfather, the Social Gospel theologian Walter Rauschenbusch. An ally of Ely and Croly, Rauschenbusch preached against those he described as "servants of Mammon . . . who drain their fellow men for gain, . . . who have made us ashamed of our dear country by their defilements, . . . [and] who have cloaked their extortion with the gospel of Christ."[21]

Because Rauschenbusch had remained a pacifist even after America's entry into World War I, because my father had been an unarmed stretcher-bearer in that war, and because one of my uncles had been staff director of the Nye Committee's investigation of the "merchants of death" in the mid-Thirties, I associated leftism with antimilitarism. But even though my father had, like John Dewey and Norman Thomas, opposed America's entry into World War II, I rejoiced that we had fought and won the war against Hitler. Because my father had once been thrown in jail for reporting on a strike, I associated the police with the goon squads who, in those days, were still being regularly hired to beat up strikers. I thought of the strikers in the coal fields and the steel mills as the great heroes of my time. When the Taft-Hartley Labor Act was passed in 1947 I could not understand how my country could have forgotten what it owed the unions, how it could fail to see that the unions had prevented America from becoming the property of the rich and greedy.

Because a lot of my relatives helped write and administer New Deal legislation, I associated leftism with a constant need for new laws and new bureaucratic initiatives which would redistribute the wealth produced by the capitalist system. I spent occasional vacations in Madison with Paul Raushenbush, who ran Wisconsin's unemployment compensation system, and his wife, Elizabeth Brandeis (a professor of labor history, and the author of the first exposé of the misery of migrant workers on

Wisconsin farms). Both were students of John R. Commons, who had passed on the heritage of his own teacher, Richard Ely. Their friends included Max Otto, a disciple of Dewey. Otto was the in-house philosopher for a group of Madison bureaucrats and academics clustered around the La Follette family. In that circle, American patriotism, redistributionist economics, anticommunism, and Deweyan pragmatism went together easily and naturally. I think of that circle as typical of the reformist American Left of the first half of the century.

Another such circle was made up of the so-called New York Intellectuals. As a teenager, I believed every anti-Stalinist word that Sidney Hook and Lionel Trilling published in *Partisan Review*—partly, perhaps, because I had been bounced on their knees as a baby. My mother used to tell me, with great pride, that when I was seven I had had the honor of serving little sandwiches to the guests at a Halloween party attended both by John Dewey and by Carlo Tresca, the Italian anarchist leader who was assassinated a few years later. That same party, I have since discovered, was attended not only by the Hooks and the Trillings, but by Whittaker Chambers. Chambers had just broken with the Communist Party and was desperately afraid of being liquidated by Stalin's hit men.[22] Another guest was Suzanne La Follette, to whom Dewey had entrusted the files of the Commission of Inquiry into the Moscow Trials. These files disappeared when her apartment was burgled, presumably by the Soviet agents.

The warnings against Stalin in Hook's and Trilling's articles were buttressed by remarks I overheard in conversations between my parents and their friends, in particular one of their neighbors: J. B. S. Hardman, an official of the Amalgamated Clothing Workers of America. Hardman had been revolutionary governor of Odessa in the 1905 Revolution, and had come to America to escape the Cheka and to organize the workers. It was in Hardman's house that I first heard of the Katyn Forest massacre, and of Stalin's murder of the Polish trade union leaders Ehrlich and Alter.

Growing up with the image of Stalin that such conversations produced, I did not find it surprising when my father, toward the end of World War II, helped Norman Thomas organize the Post-War World Council. The aim of this organization was to publicize what Stalin was preparing to do to central Europe, and to warn Americans that the wartime alliance with the USSR should not be allowed to carry over into the postwar period. The council did its best both to incite the Cold War and to prevent the American Right from monopolizing anticommunism. The latter aim was shared by a subsequent organization, the Americans for Democratic Action—an outfit slapped together in 1948 by Eleanor Roosevelt, Arthur Schlesinger, Walter Reuther, and others to counter the Communist-backed candidacy of Henry Wallace.

Inciting the Cold War struck me as continuous with the rest of the good work being done by my family and their

friends, and it still does. I am still unable to see much difference between fighting Hitler and fighting Stalin. I still find
nothing absurd in the idea that, if the reformist Left had been
stronger than it was, post–World War II America could have
had it both ways. Our country could have become both the
leader of an international movement to replace oligarchy
with social democracy around the world, and the nuclear su-
perpower which halted the spread of an evil empire ruled by
a mad tyrant.

When it was revealed, in 1967, that one of the organiza-
tions with which Thomas, Hook, Trilling, and my father
were associated—the Congress for Cultural Freedom—had
received CIA money, I was neither surprised nor appalled. It
seemed to me perfectly predictable that the CIA should contain both rightist hirelings of the United Fruit Company (the
people who had gotten Eisenhower to order the overthrow
of Colonel Arbenz—the leftist leader of Guatemala—in
1952) and leftist good guys who used the taxpayers' money
to finance what Christopher Lasch was to describe disdain-
fully as the "Cultural Cold War." The cohabitation of bad
guys with good guys in the CIA seemed to me no more surprising than that the Labor and Commerce Departments con-
tained some bureaucrats who conspired with the capitalists
against labor, and other bureaucrats who conspired with the
unions against the bosses. When in 1967 Lasch triumphantly
proclaimed that the CIA's connection with the pre-Sixties

Left showed how bankrupt the reformist Left had proved to be, I could not see what he was making such a fuss about.

So much for autobiography. I hope that I have given you some sense of what it was like to take for granted that one could be both a fervent anticommunist and a good leftist, and of the distrust with which I read books like Lasch's *The Agony of the American Left*. This was and is a very influential book, written by a distinguished scholar who was also a very useful social critic. Despite its author's intellectual and moral virtues, however, his book helped propagate the false idea that when the student Left burst into the headlines in the early Sixties, it replaced a discredited older Left.

Lasch began his book with the following quotation from Paul Goodman: "We now have the abnormal situation that there is no persuasive program for social reconstruction, thought up by many minds, corrected by endless criticism, made practical by much political activity . . . The young are honorable, and see the problems, but they don't know anything because we have not taught them anything." Lasch noted that Goodman attributed the absence of a persuasive program to "the failure of the intellectuals during the late forties and fifties." Lasch went on to say: "It is true that the defection of intellectuals in the period just past is the immediate cause of our troubles . . . My experience and the experience of many of my friends and contemporaries fully bears out the contention that the intellectuals' acquiescence in the premises of the cold war made it unusually difficult to get a political education in the fifties." However, he continued, "The deeper explanation of the present crisis of radicalism . . . lies in events that happened in the early part of the century. It lies in the collapse of mass-based radical movements which grew up for a time, and then aborted: populism, socialism, and black nationalism."[23] Lasch proceeded to dismiss the period between 1910 and 1964, the period which I think of as American leftism at its best. "Even when they originated in humanitarian impulses," Lasch wrote, "progressive ideas led not to a philosophy of liberation but to a blueprint for control . . . Manipulative and managerial, twentieth-century liberalism has adapted itself without difficulty to the corporation's need to soften conflicts."[24]

Lasch was no Marxist, but his ideas about the elites and masses paralleled those of the Marxists. Lasch thought that a movement which is not mass-based must somehow be a fraud, and that top-down initiatives are automatically suspect. This belief echoes the Marxist cult of the proletariat, the belief that there is virtue only among the oppressed. Lasch brushed aside fifty years' worth of off-and-on cooperation between the elites and the oppressed. He thereby encouraged the New Leftists' delusion that they were the first real leftists America had seen in a long time, or at least the only ones who had not sold out.

The New Leftists gradually became convinced that the Vietnam War, and the endless humiliation inflicted on

African-Americans, were clues to something deeply wrong
with their country, and not just mistakes correctable by reforms. They wanted to hear that America was a very different
sort of place, a much worse place, than their parents and
teachers had told them it was. So they responded enthusiasti-
cally to Lasch's claim that "the structure of American society
makes it almost impossible for criticism of existing policies
to become part of political discourse. The language of American politics increasingly resembles an Orwellian monologue."[25]

When they read in Lasch's book that "the United States of
the mid-twentieth century might better be described as an
empire than as a community,"[26] the students felt justified in
giving up their parents' hope that reformist politics could
cope with the injustice they saw around them. Lasch's book
made it easy to stop thinking of oneself as a member of a
community, as a citizen with civic responsibilities. For if you
turn out to be living in an evil empire (rather than, as you had
been told, a democracy fighting an evil empire), then you
have no responsibility to your country; you are accountable
only to humanity. If what your government and your teachers are saying is all part of the same Orwellian monologue—
if the differences between the Harvard faculty and the
military-industrial complex, or between Lyndon Johnson
and Barry Goldwater, are negligible—then you have a responsibility to make a revolution.

In saying things which the young leftists of the late Sixties wanted to hear, Lasch was not playing to the crowd. He was as harsh on the New Left as he was on every other aspect of contemporary America. But his writing, along with that of Goodman, Mills, and others, reconfirmed the leftist students' impression that there was nothing in America on which they could rely, except perhaps the most militant of the African-American protest movements. So they started to look for moral and intellectual support in the wrong places—the China of Mao-Tse Tung, for example. They reasoned that, since anti-Communism was the dominant theme of the Orwellian monologue Lasch described, the only way to escape from this monologue was to appreciate the achievements of the Communists. Michael Harrington's argument—that there was no reason the student Left should not also be an anticommunist Left—went unheard.[27]

The heirs of that student Left and the heirs of the older, reformist Left are still unreconciled with one another. I want to suggest that such a reconciliation could be started by agreeing that the New Left accomplished something enormously important, something of which the reformist Left would probably have been incapable. It ended the Vietnam War. It may have saved our country from becoming a garrison state. Without the widespread and continued civil disobedience conducted by the New Left, we might still be sending our young people off to kill Vietnamese, rather than expanding our overseas markets by bribing kleptocratic Communists in Ho Chi Minh City. Without the storm that broke on the campuses after the invasion of Cambodia, we might now be fighting in the farther reaches of Asia. For suppose that no young Americans had protested—that all the young men had dutifully trotted off, year after year after year, to be killed in the name of anti-Communism. Can we be so sure that the war's mere unwinnability would have been enough to persuade our government to make peace?

America will always owe an enormous amount to the rage which rumbled through the country between 1964 and 1972. We do not know what our country would be like today, had that rage not been felt. But we can be pretty certain that it would be a much worse place than it is. The CIA would undoubtedly be even more of a loose cannon than it is now. It is even possible that the Defense Department might lie to the public more frequently and fluently than at present, though I admit that this is hard to imagine. The anti-anti-Communism of the New Left, and its counterproductive habit of spelling "America" with a "k," are not important in comparison to what it achieved. By saving us from the Vietnam War, the New Left may have saved us from losing our moral identity.

It would be pointless to debate whether the New Leftists were justified in breaking with the reformist Left, and with the hope of participating in ordinary old-fashioned reformist politics, by the events of 1964–1966. There is no way to decide whether their patience should have run out in those years, rather than earlier or later. But if their patience had not run out at *some* point, if they had *never* taken to the streets, if civil disobedience had *never* replaced an insistence on working within the system, America might no longer be a constitutional democracy. Their loss of patience was the result of perfectly justified, wholly sincere moral indignation—moral indignation which, the New Left rightly sensed, we reformists were too tired and too battered to feel.

For reformers like Walter Reuther, seating the white delegates from Mississippi in the 1964 Democratic Convention was, despite the outrageous insult to the incredibly brave African-Americans who had contested those seats, justified by the need to keep the South voting Democratic.[28] The reformers were divided as to whether the Tonkin Gulf Resolution was just one more example of the spinelessness of Congress or rather a prudent attempt to give President Johnson room to maneuver. But Gitlin may be right that for the New Left these two events were the last straws. There had to be a last straw sooner or later if American leftism was ever to be revitalized. The New Left was right to say that America was in danger of selling its soul in order to defeat Communism. Even if one agrees with me in thinking that the Cold War was a necessary war, that does nothing to diminish the service which the New Left did for our country.

American leftism was revived in the 1960s by calls for revolution which, fortunately, were not successful. They did, however, lead to reform—to the passage of the legislation which Johnson rammed through Congress after being elected in 1964, and, eventually, to the withdrawal of our troops. These successes are a sufficient excuse for the Left's many and varied stupidities—even for what Paul Berman has called its "slightly crazy attempt to raise insubordination into a culture."[29] Analogously, the labor movement did succeed in getting American workers a forty-hour week and some collective-bargaining rights. This is quite enough to excuse the many instances of venal corruption in the unions and of insouciant featherbedding, which rightists prefer to dwell on. When compared with the ruthless greed, systematic corruption, and cynical deceit of the military-industrial establishment, both the New Left and the American labor movement look very good indeed.

But the old-timey Trotskyites and the people whom Lasch called "managerial liberals"—the Howes and the Schlesingers, the Hooks and the Galbraiths—do not look so bad either. A battered and exhausted Left, a Left too tired to experience rage when only rage will work, and too chastened by knowledge of the results of revolutions elsewhere to urge a revolution in America, is not the same as a Left that has sold out or become discredited.

Lasch was simply wrong when he said that it was hard to get a political education in the Fifties because of "intellectuals' acquiescence in the premises of the cold war." My friends and I got an admirable leftist education in that decade from such books as Schlesinger's *The Vital Center* and Galbraith's *The Affluent Society*. Paul Goodman was simply wrong when he said that there was no "persuasive program for social reconstruction, thought up by many minds," available for the inspection of the young in the Forties and Fifties. He can be thought right only if one takes the phrase "program for social reconstruction" to mean a proposal for revolution, rather than a list of reforms.

As I see it, the honors should be evenly divided between the older, reformist Left and the New Left of the Sixties. The heirs of that older Left should stop reminding themselves of the stupid and self-destructive things the New Left did and said toward the end of that decade. Those who are nostalgic for the Sixties should stop reminding themselves that Schlesinger lied about the Bay of Pigs and that Hook voted for Nixon. All of us should take pride in a country whose historians will someday honor the achievements of both of these Lefts.

A CULTURAL

LEFT

THE REFORMIST American Left of the first two-thirds of the century accomplished a lot. But most of the direct beneficiaries of its initiatives were white males. After women won the right to vote, the male reformers pretty much forgot about them for forty years. Right up through the early Sixties, male leftists in the hiring halls and faculty lounges often spoke of women with the same jocular contempt, and of homosexuals with the same brutal contempt, as did male rightists in the country clubs. The situation of African-Americans was deplored, but not changed, by this predominantly white Left. The Democratic Party depended on the Solid South, and Franklin D. Roosevelt had no intention of alienating Southern white voters in order to help blacks. Trade union leaders like the Reuther brothers, who desperately wanted to integrate the unions, could not do much to diminish racial prejudice among the rank and file. Black Americans began to get a semblance of decent treatment only in the 1950s, when they started taking matters into their own hands.

Most leftist reformers of this period were blissfully unaware that brown-skinned Americans in the Southwest were being lynched, segregated, and humiliated in the same way as were African-Americans in the Deep South. Almost nobody in the pre-Sixties Left thought to protest against homophobia, so leftists like F. O. Matthiessen and Bayard Rustin had to stay in the closet. From the point of view of today's Left, the pre-Sixties Left may seem as callous about the needs of oppressed groups as was the nation as a whole.

But it was not really that bad. For the reformist Left hoped that the mistreatment of the weak by the strong in general, and racial discrimination in particular, would prove to be a by-product of economic injustice. They saw the sadistic humiliation of black Americans, and of other groups, as one more example of the selfishness which pervaded an unreformed capitalist economy. They saw prejudice against those groups as incited by the rich in order to keep the poor from turning their wrath on their economic oppressors. The pre-Sixties Left assumed that as economic inequality and insecurity decreased, prejudice would gradually disappear.

In retrospect, this belief that ending selfishness would eliminate sadism seems misguided. One of the good things which happened in the Sixties was that the American Left began to realize that its economic determinism had been too simplistic. Sadism was recognized as having deeper roots than economic insecurity. The delicious pleasure to be had from creating a class of putative inferiors and then humiliating individual members of that class was seen as Freud saw it—as something which would be relished even if everybody were rich.

With this partial substitution of Freud for Marx as a source of social theory, sadism rather than selfishness has become the principal target of the Left. The heirs of the New Left of the Sixties have created, within the academy, a cultural Left. Many members of this Left specialize in what they call the "politics of difference" or "of identity" or "of recognition." This cultural Left thinks more about stigma than about money, more about deep and hidden psychosexual motivations than about shallow and evident greed.

This shift of attention came at the same time that intellectuals began to lose interest in the labor unions, partly as a result of resentment over the union members' failure to back George McGovern over Richard Nixon in 1972. Simultaneously, the leftist ferment which had been centered, before the Sixties, in the social science departments of the colleges and the universities moved into the literature departments. The study of philosophy—mostly apocalyptic French and German philosophy—replaced that of political economy as an essential preparation for participation in leftist initiatives.

The new cultural Left which has resulted from these changes has few ties to what remains of the pre-Sixties reformist Left. That saving remnant consists largely of labor lawyers and labor organizers, congressional staffers, low-level bureaucrats hoping to rescue the welfare state from the Republicans, journalists, social workers, and people who work for foundations. These are the people who worry about the way in which the practices of the National Labor Relations Board changed under the Reagan administration, about the details of alternative proposals for universal health care, about budgetary constraints on Head Start and daycare programs, and about the reversion of welfare programs to state and local governments. This residual reformist Left thinks more about laws that need to be passed than about a culture that needs to be changed.

The difference between this residual Left and the academic Left is the difference between the people who read books like Thomas Geoghegan's *Which Side Are You On?*—a brilliant explanation of how unions get busted—and people who read Fredric Jameson's *Postmodernism, or The Cultural Logic of Late Capitalism.* The latter is an equally brilliant book, but it operates on a level of abstraction too high to encourage any particular political initiative. After reading Geoghegan, you have views on some of the things which need to be done. After reading Jameson, you have views on practically everything except what needs to be done.

The academic, cultural Left approves—in a rather distant and lofty way—of the activities of these surviving reformists. But it retains a conviction which solidified in the late Sixties. It thinks that the system, and not just the laws, must be changed. Reformism is not good enough. Because the very vocabulary of liberal politics is infected with dubious presuppositions which need to be exposed, the first task of the Left must be, just as Confucius said, the rectification of names. The concern to do what the Sixties called "naming the system" takes precedence over reforming the laws.

"The system" is sometimes identified as "late capitalism," but the cultural Left does not think much about what the alternatives to a market economy might be, or about how to combine political freedom with centralized economic decisionmaking. Nor does it spend much time asking whether Americans are undertaxed, or how much of a welfare state the country can afford, or whether the United States should back out of the North American Free Trade Agreement. When the Right proclaims that socialism has failed, and that capitalism is the only alternative, the cultural Left has little to say in reply. For it prefers not to talk about money. Its principal enemy is a mind-set rather than a set of economic arrangements—a way of thinking which is, supposedly, at the root of both selfishness and sadism. This way of thinking is sometimes called "Cold War ideology," sometimes "technocratic rationality," and sometimes "phallogocentrism" (the cultural Left comes up with fresh sobriquets every year). It is a mind-set nurtured by the patriarchal and capitalist institutions of the industrial West, and its bad effects are most clearly visible in the United States.

To subvert this way of thinking, the academic Left believes, we must teach Americans to recognize otherness. To this end, leftists have helped to put together such academic disciplines as women's history, black history, gay studies, Hispanic-American studies, and migrant studies. This has led Stefan Collini to remark that in the United States, though not in Britain, the term "cultural studies" means "victim studies." Collini's choice of phrase has been resented, but he was

making a good point: namely, that such programs were created not out of the sort of curiosity about diverse forms of
human life which gave rise to cultural anthropology, but
rather from a sense of what America needed in order to make
itself a better place. The principal motive behind the new directions taken in scholarship in the United States since the
Sixties has been the urge to do something for people who
have been humiliated—to help victims of socially acceptable forms of sadism by making such sadism no longer acceptable.

Whereas the top-down initiatives of the Old Left had tried
to help people who were humiliated by poverty and unemployment, or by what Richard Sennett has called the "hidden
injuries of class," the top-down initiatives of the post-Sixties
left have been directed toward people who are humiliated for
reasons other than economic status. Nobody is setting up a
program in unemployed studies, homeless studies, or trailer-
park studies, because the unemployed, the homeless, and
residents of trailer parks are not "other" in the relevant sense.
To be other in this sense you must bear an ineradicable
stigma, one which makes you a victim of socially accepted
sadism rather than merely of economic selfishness.[1]

This cultural Left has had extraordinary success. In addi-
tion to being centers of genuinely original scholarship, the
new academic programs have done what they were, semiconsciously, designed to do: they have decreased the amount

of sadism in our society. Especially among college graduates, the casual infliction of humiliation is much less socially acceptable than it was during the first two-thirds of the century. The tone in which educated men talk about women, and educated whites about blacks, is very different from what it was before the Sixties. Life for homosexual Americans, beleaguered and dangerous as it still is, is better than it was before Stonewall. The adoption of attitudes which the Right sneers at as "politically correct" has made America a far more civilized society than it was thirty years ago.[2] Except for a few Supreme Court decisions, there has been little change for the better in our country's laws since the Sixties. But the change in the way we treat one another has been enormous.

This change is largely due to the hundreds of thousands of teachers who have done their best to make their students understand the humiliation which previous generations of Americans have inflicted on their fellow citizens. By assigning Toni Morrison's *Beloved* instead of George Eliot's *Silas Marner* in high school literature classes, and by assigning stories about the suicides of gay teenagers in freshman composition courses, these teachers have made it harder for their students to be sadistic than it was for those students' parents. By favoring women in academic hiring and preferment, and by encouraging writing about the subjugation of women, colleges and universities have helped change the relations between men and women throughout American society. It is still easy to be humiliated for being a woman in America, but such humiliation is not as frequent as it was thirty years ago.

The American academy has done as much to overcome sadism during the last thirty years as it did to overcome self-ishness in the previous seventy. Encouraging students to be what mocking neoconservatives call "politically correct" has made our country a far better place. American leftist academics have a lot to be proud of. Their conservative critics, who have no remedies to propose either for American sadism or for American selfishness, have a great deal to be ashamed of.

What these critics condemn as the politicizing of the universities is an expression of the same outrage against cruelty which moved the students and faculty of Charles University in Prague to resist the Communists in 1948, and the students and faculty at South African universities to resist apartheid laws. All universities worthy of the name have always been centers of social protest. If American universities ever cease to be such centers, they will lose both their self-respect and the respect of the learned world. It is doubtful whether the current critics of the universities who are called "conservative intellectuals" deserve this description. For intellectuals are supposed to be aware of, and speak to, issues of social justice. But even the most learned and thoughtful of current conservatives ridicule those who raise such issues. They themselves have nothing to say about whether children in the ghettos can be saved without raising suburbanites' taxes, or about how people who earn the minimum wage can pay for adequate housing. They seem to regard discussion of such topics as in poor taste.

Nevertheless, there is a dark side to the success story I have been telling about the post-Sixties cultural Left. During the same period in which socially accepted sadism has steadily diminished, economic inequality and economic insecurity have steadily increased. It is as if the American Left could not handle more than one initiative at a time—as if it either had to ignore stigma in order to concentrate on money, or vice versa.

One symptom of this inability to do two things at once is that it has been left to scurrilous demagogues like Patrick Buchanan to take political advantage of the widening gap between rich and poor. While the Left's back was turned, the bourgeoisification of the white proletariat which began in World War II and continued up through the Vietnam War has been halted, and the process has gone into reverse. America is now proletarianizing its bourgeoisie, and this process is likely to culminate in a bottom-up populist revolt, of the sort Buchanan hopes to foment.

Since 1973, the assumption that all hardworking American married couples would be able to afford a home, and that the wife could then, if she chose, stay home and raise kids, has begun to seem absurd. The question now is whether the average married couple, both working full time, will ever be able to take home more than $30,000 a year. If husband and wife each work 2,000 hours a year for the current average wage of production and nonsupervisory workers ($7.50 per hour), they will make that much. But $30,000 a year will not permit homeownership or buy decent daycare. In a country that believes neither in public transportation nor in national health insurance, this income permits a family of four only a humiliating, hand-to-mouth existence. Such a family, trying to get by on this income, will be constantly tormented by fears of wage rollbacks and downsizing, and of the disastrous consequences of even a brief illness.[3]

Seventy-two percent of Americans now think that "layoffs and loss of jobs in this country will continue indefinitely."[4] They have good reason to think this. Unless something very unexpected happens, economic insecurity will continue to grow in America. Indeed, it is easy to imagine things getting much worse much faster. This is because a good deal of the insecurity is due to the globalization of the labor market—a trend which can reasonably be expected to accelerate indefinitely.

What industrialization was to America at the end of the nineteenth century, globalization is at the end of the twentieth. The problem which Dewey and Croly faced—how to prevent wage-slavery from destroying the hope of equality—was partly solved by the leftist initiatives of 1910–1965. But a problem Dewey and Croly never envisaged has taken its place, and measures which might cope with this new problem have hardly even been sketched. The problem is that the wage levels, and the social benefits, enjoyed by workers in Europe, Japan, and North America no longer bear any relation to the newly fluid global labor market.

Globalization is producing a world economy in which an attempt by any one country to prevent the immiseration of its workers may result only in depriving them of employment. This world economy will soon be owned by a cosmopolitan upper class which has no more sense of community with any workers anywhere than the great American capitalists of the year 1900 had with the immigrants who manned their enterprises. The increasing dependence of American universities on gifts from abroad, of American political parties on bribes from abroad, and of the American economy on foreign sales of Treasury bonds are examples of the tendencies which are at work.

This frightening economic cosmopolitanism has, as a by-product, an agreeable cultural cosmopolitanism. Platoons of vital young entrepreneurs fill the front cabins of transoceanic jets, while the back cabins are weighted down with paunchy professors like myself, zipping off to interdisciplinary conferences held in pleasant places.[5] But this newly-acquired cultural cosmopolitanism is limited to the richest twenty-five percent of Americans. The new economic cosmopolitanism presages a future in which the other 75 percent of Americans will find their standard of living steadily shrinking. We are likely to wind up with an America divided into hereditary social castes. This America will be run by what Michael Lind (in *The Next American Nation*) has called the "overclass," the highly educated and expensively groomed top 25 percent. One of the scariest social trends is illustrated by the fact that in 1979 kids from the top socioeconomic quarter of American families were four times more likely to get a college degree than those from the bottom quarter; now they are ten times more likely.[6]

It is as if, sometime around 1980, the children of the people who made it through the Great Depression and into the suburbs had decided to pull up the drawbridge behind them. They decided that although social mobility had been appropriate for their parents, it was not to be allowed to the next generation. These suburbanites seem to see nothing wrong with belonging to a hereditary caste, and have initiated what Robert Reich (in his book *The Work of Nations*) calls "the secession of the successful."

Sometime in the Seventies, American middle-class idealism went into a stall. Under Presidents Carter and Clinton, the Democratic Party has survived by distancing itself from the unions and from any mention of redistribution, and moving into a sterile vacuum called the "center." The party no longer has a visible, noisy left wing—a wing with which the intellectuals can identify and on which the unions can rely for support. It is as if the distribution of income and wealth had become too scary a topic for any American politician—much less any sitting president—ever to mention. Politicians fear that mentioning it would lose them votes among the only Americans who can be relied on to go to the polls: the suburbanites. So the choice between the two major parties has come down to a choice between cynical lies and terrified silence.

If the formation of hereditary castes continues unimpeded, and if the pressures of globalization create such castes not only in the United States but in all the old democracies, we shall end up in an Orwellian world. In such a world, there may be no supernational analogue of Big Brother, or any official creed analogous to Ingsoc. But there will be an analogue of the Inner Party—namely, the international, cosmopolitan super-rich. They will make all the important decisions. The analogue of Orwell's Outer Party will be educated, comfortably off, cosmopolitan professionals—Lind's "overclass," the people like you and me.

The job of people like us will be to make sure that the decisions made by the Inner Party are carried out smoothly and efficiently. It will be in the interest of the international super-rich to keep our class relatively prosperous and happy. For they need people who can pretend to be the political class of each of the individual nation-states. For the sake of keeping the proles quiet, the super-rich will have to keep up the pretense that national politics might someday make a difference. Since economic decisions are their prerogative, they will encourage politicians, of both the Left and the Right, to specialize in cultural issues.[7] The aim will be to keep the minds of the proles elsewhere—to keep the bottom 75 percent of Americans and the bottom 95 percent of the world's population busy with ethnic and religious hostilities, and with debates about sexual mores. If the proles can be distracted from their own despair by media-created pseudo-events, including the occasional brief and bloody war, the super-rich will have little to fear.

Contemplation of this possible world invites two responses from the Left. The first is to insist that the inequalities between nations need to be mitigated—and, in particular, that the Northern Hemisphere must share its wealth with the Southern. The second is to insist that the primary responsibility of each democratic nation-state is to its own least advantaged citizens. These two responses obviously conflict with each other. In particular, the first response suggests that the old democracies should open their borders, whereas the second suggests that they should close them.[8]

The first response comes naturally to academic leftists, who have always been internationally minded. The second response comes naturally to members of trade unions, and to the marginally employed people who can most easily be recruited into right-wing populist movements. Union members in the United States have watched factory after factory close, only to reopen in Slovenia, Thailand, or Mexico. It is no wonder that they see the result of international free trade as prosperity for managers and stockholders, a better standard of living for workers in developing countries, and a very much worse standard of living for American workers. It would be no wonder if they saw the American leftist intelligentsia as on the side of the managers and stockholders—as sharing the same class interests. For we intellectuals, who are mostly academics, are ourselves quite well insulated, at least in the short run, from the effects of globalization. To make things worse, we often seem more interested in the workers of the developing world than in the fate of our fellow citizens.

Many writers on socioeconomic policy have warned that the old industrialized democracies are heading into a Weimar-like period, one in which populist movements are likely to overturn constitutional governments. Edward Luttwak, for example, has suggested that fascism may be the American future. The point of his book *The Endangered American Dream* is that members of labor unions, and unorganized unskilled workers, will sooner or later realize that their government is not even trying to prevent wages from sinking or to prevent jobs from being exported. Around the same time, they will realize that suburban white-collar workers—themselves desperately afraid of being downsized—are not going to let themselves be taxed to provide social benefits for anyone else.

At that point, something will crack. The nonsuburban electorate will decide that the system has failed and start looking around for a strongman to vote for—someone willing to assure them that, once he is elected, the smug bureaucrats, tricky lawyers, overpaid bond salesmen, and postmodernist professors will no longer be calling the shots. A scenario like that of Sinclair Lewis' novel It Can't Happen Here may then be played out. For once such a strongman takes office, nobody can predict what will happen. In 1932, most of the predictions made about what would happen if Hindenburg named Hitler chancellor were wildly overoptimistic.

One thing that is very likely to happen is that the gains made in the past forty years by black and brown Americans, and by homosexuals, will be wiped out. Jocular contempt for women will come back into fashion. The words "nigger" and "kike" will once again be heard in the workplace. All the sadism which the academic Left has tried to make unacceptable to its students will come flooding back. All the resentment which badly educated Americans feel about having their manners dictated to them by college graduates will find an outlet.

But such a renewal of sadism will not alter the effects of selfishness. For after my imagined strongman takes charge, he will quickly make his peace with the international super-rich, just as Hitler made his with the German industrialists. He will invoke the glorious memory of the Gulf War to provoke military adventures which will generate short-term prosperity. He will be a disaster for the country and the world. People will wonder why there was so little resistance to his evitable rise. Where, they will ask, was the American Left? Why was it only rightists like Buchanan who spoke to the workers about the consequences of globalization? Why could not the Left channel the mounting rage of the newly dispossessed?

It is often said that we Americans, at the end of the twentieth century, no longer have a Left. Since nobody denies the existence of what I have called the cultural Left, this amounts to an admission that that Left is unable to engage in national politics. It is not the sort of Left which can be asked to deal with the consequences of globalization. To get the country to deal with those consequences, the present cultural Left would have to transform itself by opening relations with the residue of the old reformist Left, and in particular with the labor unions. It would have to talk much more about money, even at the cost of talking less about stigma.

I have two suggestions about how to effect this transition. The first is that the Left should put a moratorium on theory. It should try to kick its philosophy habit. The second is that the Left should try to mobilize what remains of our pride in being Americans. It should ask the public to consider how the country of Lincoln and Whitman might be achieved.

In support of my first suggestion, let me cite a passage from Dewey's *Reconstruction in Philosophy* in which he expresses his exasperation with the sort of sterile debate now going on under the rubric of "individualism versus communitarianism." Dewey thought that all discussions which took this dichotomy seriously

> suffer from a common defect. They are all committed to the logic of general notions under which specific situations are to be brought. What we want is light upon this or that group of individuals, this or that concrete human being, this or that special institution or social arrangement. For such a logic of inquiry, the traditionally accepted logic substitutes discussion of the meaning of concepts and their dialectical relationships with one another.

Dewey was right to be exasperated by sociopolitical theory conducted at this level of abstraction. He was wrong when he went on to say that ascending to this level is typically a right-ist maneuver, one which supplies "the apparatus for intellectual justifications of the established order."[9] For such ascents are now more common on the Left than on the Right. The contemporary academic Left seems to think that the higher your level of abstraction, the more subversive of the established order you can be. The more sweeping and novel your conceptual apparatus, the more radical your critique.

When one of today's academic leftists says that some topic has been "inadequately theorized," you can be pretty certain that he or she is going to drag in either philosophy of language, or Lacanian psychoanalysis, or some neo-Marxist version of economic determinism. Theorists of the Left think that dissolving political agents into plays of differential subjectivity, or political initiatives into pursuits of Lacan's impossible object of desire, helps to subvert the established order. Such subversion, they say, is accomplished by "problematizing familiar concepts."

Recent attempts to subvert social institutions by problematizing concepts have produced a few very good books. They have also produced many thousands of books which represent scholastic philosophizing at its worst. The authors of these purportedly "subversive" books honestly believe that they are serving human liberty. But it is almost impossible to clamber back down from their books to a level of abstraction on which one might discuss the merits of a law, a treaty, a candidate, or a political strategy. Even though what these authors "theorize" is often something very concrete and near at hand—a current TV show, a media celebrity, a recent scandal—they offer the most abstract and barren explanations imaginable.

These futile attempts to philosophize one's way into political relevance are a symptom of what happens when a Left re-
treats from activism and adopts a spectatorial approach to the
problems of its country. Disengagement from practice produces theoretical hallucinations. These result in an intellectual environment which is, as Mark Edmundson says in his
book *Nightmare on Main Street*, Gothic. The cultural Left is
haunted by ubiquitous specters, the most frightening of
which is called "power." This is the name of what Edmundson calls Foucault's "haunting agency, which is everywhere
and nowhere, as evanescent and insistent as a resourceful
spook."[10]

In its Foucauldian usage, the term "power" denotes an
agency which has left an indelible stain on every word in our
language and on every institution in our society. It is always
already there, and cannot be spotted coming or going. One
might spot a corporate bagman arriving at a congressman's
office, and perhaps block his entrance. But one cannot block
off power in the Foucauldian sense. Power is as much inside
one as outside one. It is nearer than hands and feet. As Edmundson says: one cannot "confront power; one can only
encounter its temporary and generally unwitting agents . . .
[it] has capacities of motion and transformation that make it
a *preternatural* force."[11] Only interminable individual and social self-analysis, and perhaps not even that, can help us escape from the infinitely fine meshes of its invisible web.

The ubiquity of Foucauldian power is reminiscent of the ubiquity of Satan, and thus of the ubiquity of original sin—that diabolical stain on every human soul. I argued in my first lecture that the repudiation of the concept of sin was at the heart of Dewey and Whitman's civic religion. I also claimed that the American Left, in its horror at the Vietnam War, reinvented sin. It reinvented the old religious idea that some stains are ineradicable. I now wish to say that, in committing itself to what it calls "theory," this Left has gotten something which is entirely too much like religion. For the cultural Left has come to believe that we must place our country within a theoretical frame of reference, situate it within a vast quasi-cosmological perspective.

Stories about the webs of power and the insidious influence of a hegemonic ideology do for this Left what stories about the Lamanites did for Joseph Smith and what stories about Yakkub did for Elijah Muhammad. What stories about blue-eyed devils are to the Black Muslims, stories about hegemony and power are to many cultural leftists—the only thing they really want to hear. To step into the intellectual world which some of these leftists inhabit is to move out of a world in which the citizens of a democracy can join forces to resist sadism and selfishness into a Gothic world in which democratic politics has become a farce. It is a world in which all the daylit cheerfulness of Whitmanesque hypersecularism has been lost, and in which "liberalism" and "humanism" are synonyms for naiveté—for an inability to grasp the full horror of our situation.

I have argued in various books that the philosophers most often cited by cultural leftists—Nietzsche, Heidegger, Foucault, and Derrida—are largely right in their criticisms of Enlightenment rationalism. I have argued further that traditional liberalism and traditional humanism are entirely compatible with such criticisms. We can still be old-fashioned reformist liberals even if, like Dewey, we give up the correspondence theory of truth and start treating moral and scientific beliefs as tools for achieving greater human happiness, rather than as representations of the intrinsic nature of reality. We can be this kind of liberal even after we turn our backs on Descartes, linguistify subjectivity, and see everything around us and within us as one more replaceable social construction.

But I have also urged that insofar as these antimetaphysical, anti-Cartesian philosophers offer a quasi-religious form of spiritual pathos, they should be relegated to private life and not taken as guides to political deliberation. The notion of "infinite responsibility," formulated by Emmanuel Levinas and sometimes deployed by Derrida—as well as Derrida's own frequent discoveries of impossibility, unreachability, and unrepresentability—may be useful to some of us in our individual quests for private perfection. When we take up our public responsibilities, however, the infinite and the unrepresentable are merely nuisances. Thinking of our responsibilities in these terms is as much of a stumbling-block to effective political organization as is the sense of sin. Emphasizing the impossibility of meaning, or of justice, as Derrida sometimes does, is a temptation to Gothicize—to view democratic politics as ineffectual, because unable to cope with preternatural forces.

Whitman and Dewey, I have argued, gave us all the romance, and all the spiritual uplift, we Americans need to go about our public business. As Edmundson remarks, we should not allow Emerson, who was a precursor of both Whitman and Dewey, to be displaced by Poe, who was a precursor of Lacan. For purposes of thinking about how to achieve our country, we do not need to worry about the correspondence theory of truth, the grounds of normativity, the impossibility of justice, or the infinite distance which separates us from the other. For those purposes, we can give both religion and philosophy a pass. We can just get on with trying to solve what Dewey called "the problems of men."

To think about those problems means to refrain from thinking so much about otherness that we begin to acquiesce in what Todd Gitlin has called, in the title of a recent book, "the twilight of common dreams." It means deriving our moral identity, at least in part, from our citizenship in a democratic nation-state, and from leftist attempts to fulfill the promise of that nation.

The cultural Left often seems convinced that the nation-state is obsolete, and that there is therefore no point in attempting to revive national politics. The trouble with this claim is that the government of our nation-state will be, for the foreseeable future, the only agent capable of making any real difference in the amount of selfishness and sadism inflicted on Americans.

It is no comfort to those in danger of being immiserated by globalization to be told that, since national governments are now irrelevant, we must think up a replacement for such governments. The cosmopolitan super-rich do not think any replacements are needed, and they are likely to prevail. Bill Readings was right to say that "the nation-state [has ceased] to be the elemental unit of capitalism," but it remains the entity which makes decisions about social benefits, and thus about social justice.[12] The current leftist habit of taking the long view and looking beyond nationhood to a global polity is as useless as was faith in Marx's philosophy of history, for which it has become a substitute. Both are equally irrelevant to the question of how to prevent the reemergence of hereditary castes, or of how to prevent right-wing populists from taking advantage of resentment at that reemergence.

When we think about these latter questions, we begin to realize that one of the essential transformations which the cultural Left will have to undergo is the shedding of its semiconscious anti-Americanism, which it carried over from the rage of the late Sixties. This Left will have to stop thinking up ever more abstract and abusive names for "the system" and start trying to construct inspiring images of the country. Only by doing so can it begin to form alliances with people outside the academy—and, specifically, with the labor unions. Outside the academy, Americans still want to feel patriotic. They still want to feel part of a nation which can take control of its destiny and make itself a better place.

If the Left forms no such alliances, it will never have any effect on the laws of the United States. To form them will require the cultural Left to forget about Baudrillard's account of America as Disneyland—as a country of simulacra—and to start proposing changes in the laws of a real country, inhabited by real people who are enduring unnecessary suffering, much of which can be cured by governmental action.[13] Nothing would do more to resurrect the American Left than agreement on a concrete political platform, a People's Charter, a list of specific reforms. The existence of such a list—endlessly reprinted and debated, equally familiar to professors and production workers, imprinted on the memory both of professional people and of those who clean the professionals' toilets—might revitalize leftist politics.[14]

The problems which can be cured by governmental action, and which such a list would canvass, are mostly those that stem from selfishness rather than sadism. But to bring about such cures it would help if the Left would change the

tone in which it now discusses sadism. The pre-Sixties reformist Left, insofar as it concerned itself with oppressed mi-
norities, did so by proclaiming that all of us—black, white,
and brown—are Americans, and that we should respect one
another as such. This strategy gave rise to the "platoon"
movies, which showed Americans of various ethnic back-
grounds fighting and dying side by side. By contrast, the contemporary cultural Left urges that America should not be a
melting-pot, because we need to respect one another in our
differences. This Left wants to preserve otherness rather than
ignore it.

The distinction between the old strategy and the new is
important. The choice between them makes the difference
between what Todd Gitlin calls "common dreams" and what
Arthur Schlesinger calls "disuniting America." To take pride
in being black or gay is an entirely reasonable response to the
sadistic humiliation to which one has been subjected. But insofar as this pride prevents someone from also taking pride in
being an American citizen, from thinking of his or her country as capable of reform, or from being able to join with
straights or whites in reformist initiatives, it is a political
disaster.

The rhetorical question of the "platoon" movies—"What
do our differences matter, compared with our commonality
as fellow Americans?"—did not commend pride in difference, but neither did it condemn it. The intent of posing that

question was to help us become a country in which a person's difference would be largely neglected by others, unless the person in question wished to call attention to it. If the cultural Left insists on its present strategy—on asking us to respect one another in our differences rather than asking us to cease noticing those differences—it will have to find a new way of creating a sense of commonality at the level of national politics. For only a rhetoric of commonality can forge a winning majority in national elections.

I doubt that any such new way will be found. Nobody has yet suggested a viable leftist alternative to the civic religion of which Whitman and Dewey were prophets. That civic religion centered around taking advantage of traditional pride in American citizenship by substituting social justice for individual freedom as our country's principal goal. We were supposed to love our country because it showed promise of being kinder and more generous than other countries. As the blacks and the gays, among others, were well aware, this was a counsel of perfection rather than description of fact. But you cannot urge national political renewal on the basis of descriptions of fact. You have to describe the country in terms of what you passionately hope it will become, as well as in terms of what you know it to be now. You have to be loyal to a dream country rather than to the one to which you wake up every morning. Unless such loyalty exists, the ideal has no chance of becoming actual.

But the country of one's dreams must be a country one can imagine being constructed, over the course of time, by human hands. One reason the cultural Left will have a hard time transforming itself into a political Left is that, like the Sixties Left, it still dreams of being rescued by an angelic power called "the people." In this sense, "the people" is the name of a redemptive preternatural force, a force whose demonic counterpart is named "power" or "the system." The cultural Left inherited the slogan "Power to the people" from the Sixties Left, whose members rarely asked about how the transference of power was supposed to work. This question still goes unasked.

Edmundson, Delbanco, and other cultural commentators have remarked that the contemporary United States is filled with visions of demons and angels. Stephen King and Tony Kushner have helped form a national collective unconscious which is "Gothic" in Edmundson's sense. It produces dreams not of political reforms but of inexplicable, magical transformations. The cultural Left has contributed to the formation of this politically useless unconscious not only by adopting "power" as the name of an invisible, ubiquitous, and malevolent presence, but by adopting ideals which nobody is yet able to imagine being actualized.

Among these ideals are participatory democracy and the end of capitalism. Power will pass to the people, the Sixties Left believed, only when decisions are made by all those who may be affected by their results. This means, for example, that economic decisions will be made by stakeholders rather than by shareholders, and that entrepreneurship and markets will cease to play their present role. When they do, capitalism as we know it will have ended, and something new will have taken its place.

But what this new thing will be, nobody knows. The Sixties did not ask how the various groups of stakeholders were to reach a consensus about when to remodel a factory rather than build a new one, what prices to pay for raw materials, and the like. Sixties leftists skipped lightly over all the questions which had been raised by the experience of nonmarket economies in the so-called socialist countries. They seemed to be suggesting that once we were rid of both bureaucrats and entrepreneurs, "the people" would know how to handle competition from steel mills or textile factories in the developing world, price hikes on imported oil, and so on. But they never told us how "the people" would learn how to do this.

The cultural Left still skips over such questions. Doing so is a consequence of its preference for talking about "the system" rather than about specific social practices and specific changes in those practices. The rhetoric of this Left remains revolutionary rather than reformist and pragmatic. Its insouciant use of terms like "late capitalism" suggests that we can just wait for capitalism to collapse, rather than figuring out what, in the absence of markets, will set prices and regulate distribution. The voting public, the public which must be won over if the Left is to emerge from the academy into the public square, sensibly wants to be told the details. It wants to know how things are going to work after markets are put behind us. It wants to know how participatory democracy is supposed to function.

The cultural Left offers no answers to such demands for further information, but until it confronts them it will not be able to be a political Left. The public, sensibly, has no interest in getting rid of capitalism until it is offered details about the alternatives. Nor should it be interested in participatory democracy—the liberation of the people from the power of the technocrats—until it is told how deliberative assemblies will acquire the same know-how which only the technocrats presently possess. Even someone like myself, whose admiration for John Dewey is almost unlimited, cannot take seriously his defense of participatory democracy against Walter Lippmann's insistence on the need for expertise.[15]

The cultural Left has a vision of an America in which the white patriarchs have stopped voting and have left all the voting to be done by members of previously victimized groups, people who have somehow come into possession of more foresight and imagination than the selfish suburbanites. These formerly oppressed and newly powerful people are expected to be as angelic as the straight white males were diabolical. If I shared this expectation, I too would want to live under this new dispensation. Since I see no reason to share it, I think that the Left should get back into the business of piecemeal reform within the framework of a market economy. This was the business the American Left was in during the first two-thirds of the century.

Someday, perhaps, cumulative piecemeal reforms will be found to have brought about revolutionary change. Such reforms might someday produce a presently unimaginable nonmarket economy, and much more widely distributed powers of decisionmaking. They might also, given similar reforms in other countries, bring about an international federation, a world government. In such a new world, American national pride would become as quaint as pride in being from Nebraska or Kazakhstan or Sicily. But in the meantime, we should not let the abstractly described best be the enemy of the better. We should not let speculation about a totally changed system, and a totally different way of thinking about human life and human affairs, replace step-by-step reform of the system we presently have.

LET ME RETURN, yet again, to the theme with which I began: the contrast between spectatorship and agency.

From the point of view of a detached cosmopolitan spectator, our country may seem to have little to be proud of. The United States of America finally freed its slaves, but it then invented segregation laws which were as ingeniously cruel as

Hitler's Nuremberg laws. It started to create a welfare state, but quickly fell behind the rest of the industrial democracies in providing equal medical care, education, and opportunity to the children of the rich and of the poor. Its workers built a strong labor movement, but then allowed this movement to be crushed by restrictive legislation and by the gangsters whom they weakly allowed to take over many locals. Its government perverted a justified crusade against an evil empire into a conspiracy with right-wing oligarchs to suppress social democratic movements.

I have been arguing that the appropriate response to such observations is that we Americans should not take the point of view of a detached cosmopolitan spectator. We should face up to unpleasant truths about ourselves, but we should not take those truths to be the last word about our chances for happiness, or about our national character. Our national character is still in the making. Few in 1897 would have predicted the Progressive Movement, the forty-hour week, Women's Suffrage, the New Deal, the Civil Rights Movement, the successes of second-wave feminism, or the Gay Rights Movement. Nobody in 1997 can know that America will not, in the course of the next century, witness even greater moral progress.

Whitman and Dewey tried to substitute hope for knowledge. They wanted to put shared utopian dreams—dreams of an ideally decent and civilized society—in the place of knowledge of God's Will, Moral Law, the Laws of History, or the Facts of Science. Their party, the party of hope, made twentieth-century America more than just an economic and military giant. Without the American Left, we might still have been strong and brave, but nobody would have suggested that we were good. As long as we have a functioning political Left, we still have a chance to achieve our country, to make it the country of Whitman's and Dewey's dreams.

APPENDIXES

NOTES

ACKNOWLEDGMENTS

INDEX

MOVEMENTS AND
CAMPAIGNS

In 1954, the year in which he founded *Dissent*, Irving
Howe published an essay called "This Age of Conformity" in
Partisan Review. There he contrasted the dynamism of *Partisan
Review*'s glory days with the complacent passivity of the intel-
lectuals at the beginning of the Eisenhower years. Here is his
description of the avant-garde as it was:

> The achievements of Joyce, Proust, Schönberg, Bartók,
> Picasso, Matisse, to mention only the obvious figures,
> signified one of the major turnings in the cultural his-
> tory of the West, a turning made all the more crucial by
> the fact that it came not during the vigor of a society but
> during its crisis. To counter this hostility which the
> work of such artists met among all the official spokes-
> men of culture, to discover formal terms and modes
> through which to secure these achievements, to insist
> upon the continuity between their work and the ac-
> cepted, because dead, artists of the past—this became
> the task of the avant-garde. Somewhat later a section of
> the avant-garde also became politically active, and not

by accident; for precisely those aroused sensibilities that had responded to the innovations of the modern masters now responded to the crisis of modern society. Thus, in the early years of a magazine like *Partisan Review*—roughly between 1936 and 1941—these two radical impulses came together in an uneasy but fruitful union; and it was in those years that the magazine seemed most exciting and vital as a link between art and experience, between the critical consciousness and the political conscience, between the avant-garde of letters and the independent left of politics.[1]

I vaguely remember reading this essay as an eager twenty-two-year-old. At that age, I thought the end of desire was to get something published in *Partisan Review*—preferably something which would, like Irving Howe's own essays, combine critical consciousness with political conscience. Forty years ago, I probably believed every word of the passage I just quoted.

Rereading this passage now, I find that I believe very little of it. I do not think that the art and literature of the early twentieth century marked a major turning in the cultural history of the West. I doubt that the troubles of that time are even a reasonable candidate for "the crisis of modern society." Rereading Howe's later work, I realized that he probably came to believe rather little of this passage himself. Howe was too forward-looking to spend much time correcting or glossing his past writings. But by the time he wrote *A Margin of Hope*, he was much more skeptical about the very idea of a "movement" than he had been thirty years before.

In that book, written in the early 1980s, he pokes gentle fun at Philip Rahv's insistence that *Partisan Review* should "always seem to be moving somewhere," and at the "imagery of politics" which his younger self shared with Rahv: "an imagery of definition, conflict, alliance, exclusion."[2] He is mildly sardonic about William Phillips' claim in 1946 that the writers he was then publishing in *Partisan Review*—Randall Jarrell, Elizabeth Bishop, Saul Bellow, Mary McCarthy—lacked "the élan and confidence of a movement."[3] In one paragraph, indeed, he comes close to explicitly repudiating the passage I quoted earlier:

> The union of the *advanced*, much as it entranced and enabled, was an idea that could not long endure. Avant-gardes march forward, but not necessarily to the same tune or in the same direction. By the time the *Partisan* writers came along, both the literary and political avant-gardes were living off remembered glories . . . Modernism was not moving along a necessary line of purpose and progress . . . No, the union between cultural modernism and independent radicalism was neither a proper marriage nor a secure liaison; it was a meeting

between parties hurrying in opposite directions, brief, hectic, messy.[4]

What Howe says here was anticipated by his own practice in editing *Dissent*. The difference between that magazine and *Partisan Review* during its first decade is that *Dissent*, and the group of writers around it, felt able to dispense with membership in a movement. They were content simply to throw themselves into a lot of campaigns. By "campaign," I mean something finite, something that can be recognized to have succeeded or to have, so far, failed. Movements, by contrast, neither succeed nor fail. They are too big and too amorphous to do anything that simple. They share in what Kierkegaard called "the passion of the infinite." They are exemplified by Christianity and by Marxism, the sort of movements which enable novelists like Dostoevsky to do what Howe admiringly called "*feeling* thought."[5]

Membership in a movement requires the ability to see particular campaigns for particular goals as parts of something much bigger, and as having little meaning in themselves. Campaigns for such goals as the unionization of migrant farm workers, or the overthrow (by votes or by force) of a corrupt government, or socialized medicine, or legal recognition of gay marriage can be conducted without much attention to literature, art, philosophy, or history. But movements levy contributions from each of these areas of culture.

They are needed to provide a larger context within which politics is no longer just politics, but rather the matrix out of which will emerge something like Paul's "new being in Christ" or Mao's "new socialist man." Movement politics, the sort which held "bourgeois reformism" in contempt, was the kind of politics which Howe came to know all too well in the Thirties, and was doubtful about when it was reinvented in the Sixties. This kind of politics assumes that things will be changed utterly, that a terrible new beauty will be born.

Howe knew so well what it was like to belong to a movement when he was young that he was able to do without movements when he was older. So he, and the magazine he founded, were able to stick to campaigning. But of course this does not mean that he turned away from literature, art, philosophy, and history. He stayed in contact with all of these, but he no longer felt the same need to link critical consciousness with political conscience, to synthesize perfection of the work with perfection of the life. The difference between reading *Partisan Review* under Rahv and reading *Dissent* under Howe was that one read the former in order to take one's own spiritual temperature, and the latter in order to get the details on how the strong were currently oppressing the weak, how the rich were currently cheating the poor. *Partisan Review* was something to be lived up to, but *Dissent* was, and is, a source of information and advice.

In *A Margin of Hope,* Howe wrote that by the time he was thirty he knew that he wanted to "write literary criticism like that which Edmund Wilson and George Orwell wrote."[6] As he did this more and more successfully, he moved, like the two men he took as models, beyond the need to be in tune with, and faithful to, something larger than himself. Like Wilson and Orwell, he wrote as he pleased and about what he pleased, without asking which larger goals he served or how his work tied in with the spirit of the age. Like them, he was able to fight off the specter of Tolstoy by insisting that "there are kinds of beauty before which the moral imagination ought to withdraw."[7] Even though he was admittedly troubled because he could not "reconcile my desire to be a writer with remembered fantasies about public action," he was the envy of his contemporaries, precisely because he was able to find the time to be both an accomplished man of letters and the unpaid editor of his country's most useful political magazine. He managed to combine the talents and the usefulness of an Allen Tate with those of a Bayard Rustin.

Howe would have loathed being called a warrior-saint, but this term does help catch one of the reasons he came to play the role in many people's lives which Orwell had played in his. The young people who helped him with *Dissent* learned from him how one could combine the contemplative and the active lives, how to look inward and outward on alternate days of the week, and how to combine this ambidexterity with a sense of finitude and an ironic recognition of impurity.

Most of us, when young, hope for purity of heart. The easiest way to assure oneself of this purity is to will one thing—but this requires seeing everything as part of a pattern whose center is that single thing. Movements offer such a pattern, and thus offer such assurance of purity. Howe's ability, in his later decades, to retain both critical consciousness and political conscience, while not attempting to fuse the two into something larger than either, showed his admirers how to forgo such purity and such a pattern.

When literature replaces the Bible, polytheism and its problems return: choices between Tolstoy and Dostoevsky, or between Proust and Genet, replace choices between Jaweh and Baal or between Apollo and Dionysus. The prominence of the literary critic in the culture of the past two centuries is a natural consequence of the Romantic apotheosis of the creative artist: gods require contemplators of their splendor and glosses on their pronouncements. But whereas worship of One God, especially a God modeled on a Platonic Idea, requires purity of heart, polytheism requires the ability to internalize and tolerate oppositions—oppositions not just between novelists and novels, but within both.

Howe said that one of the "secrets" of the novel in general may be "the vast respect which the great novelist is ready to offer to the whole idea of *opposition*—the opposition he needs to allow for in his book against his own predispositions and yearnings and fantasies."[8] I suspect that Harold Bloom is right that this secret of the novel is the secret of literature, considered as the area of culture which finds itself in perpetual opposition to science and philosophy.[9] Literature, Bloom says, adheres to Protagoras' motto "Two logoi opposing one another," and thus is as inevitably polytheist and agonistic as Plato's invention, philosophy, is inevitably monistic and convergent. Movements are suited to onto-theological Platonists, campaigns to many-minded men of letters.

The specific sort of opposition which most interested Howe is the one described in the epigraph from Max Scheler which he chose for *Politics and the Novel*: "True tragedy arises 'when the idea of "justice" appears to be leading to the destruction of higher values.'" An aspirant to political sainthood can avoid that kind of tragedy by purifying his heart, having only one yearning and only one fantasy. Such an aspirant will repeat over and over, "Not my will, but the Movement's, be done." Part of what helped Howe turn from movements to campaigns was the lesson he learned from political novels: a lesson about the dangers of such attempts at self-purification and self-surrender. A multiplicity of campaigns has the same advantage as a plurality of gods or of novels: each campaign is finite, and there is always another campaign to enlist in when the first fails or goes rancid. The realized impurity of a movement can destroy the person who has identified himself with that movement, but the impurity of a campaign can be taken in one's stride: such impurity is just what one expects of something finite and mortal.

What Howe said of modernism is true of all movements, but of no campaigns: namely, that it "must always struggle but never quite triumph, and then, after a time, must struggle in order not to triumph."[10] If the passion of the infinite were to triumph, it would betray itself by revealing itself to have been merely a passion for something finite. Anyone who prides himself on having achieved purity of heart convicts himself out of his own mouth. So Howe raises just the right question when, at the end of his essay "The Idea of the Modern," he asks, "How, come to think of it, do great cultural movements end?"[11]

I am inclined to answer this question by saying that such a movement can be killed off only by another movement of the same kind. It takes a new sublime to kill an old sublime. As the century wore on, it became increasingly difficult for literary critics to avoid demoting "modernism" from the sublimity of a movement to the finitude of a period—to avoid saying that Proust, Picasso, and the rest were characteristic not of "the crisis of modern society," but simply of early twentieth-century art and literature, as Baudelaire and Delacroix had been characteristic of mid-nineteenth-century art and literature.

The increasing mustiness of modernism in the Fifties and Sixties caused the journals of that period to be filled with essays like Howe's—essays which tried, and uniformly failed, to offer "formal terms and modes through which to secure" the achievements of literary modernism. Eventually and inevitably such attempts were tacitly abandoned. But there were still people who could not live without a movement. So they invented a new one. They proclaimed that although the sublimity claimed by "high modernism" had, unfortunately, proved spurious, one more turn of the screw would take us from modernism to *postmodernism*, and thereby enable us to attain *true* sublimity.

Not all the books which describe themselves as dealing with "the postmodern" are up-market media hype. Gianni Vattimo's and Zygmunt Bauman's books, for example, are not. But books like Baudrillard's and Jameson's are what Vincent Descombes calls "philosophies of current events." These books are metahypes, hyping the very process of media hyping, hoping to find the essence of what's happening by examining the entrails of magazines. The readers of these books are the people who ask themselves whether the latest building, TV program, advertisement, rock group, or curriculum is properly postmodern, or whether it still betrays traces of mere modernism.

Reading such postmodern philosophies of current events leads one to wonder just how much of modernism itself was media hype. One wonders, for example, whether a good deal of Ezra Pound's critical writing may not belong, as Cyril Connolly said of Edith Sitwell's, to the history of public relations rather than that of literature. It also makes one wonder whether Howe himself did not succumb to the hype put out by Pound, Eliot, T. E. Hulme, and others, when he wrote that that period had marked "one of the major turnings in the cultural history of the West."

Such reflections suggest a more general question: What might the cultural history and sociopolitical history of the West look like if we tried to narrate both without mention of major turnings? What would they look like if they were written as the histories of a very large number of small campaigns, rather than as the history of a few great movements? What would our past look like if we decided that (in the words that Bruno Latour takes as the title of his brilliant book) "we have never been modern"—that history is an endless network of changing relationships, without any great climactic ruptures or peripeties, and that terms like "traditional society," "modern society," and "postmodern society" are more trouble than they are worth?

Let me offer some tentative answers to these questions. I suggest that the analogue of a sociopolitical campaign, such as that on behalf of the eight-hour workday or equal pay for equal work, is the career of an individual poet, novelist, dancer, critic, or painter. Such a career, like such a campaign, is finite and mortal, and can be seen to have succeeded or failed—or, more frequently, to have succeeded to a certain degree while still falling short of its initial aims. Careers, like campaigns, may borrow impetus and enthusiasm from, or may define themselves by opposition to, contemporary careers and campaigns. This is why there are artistic, as well as sociopolitical, alliances and struggles.

The reason I cite poets, critics, and painters, rather than dentists, carpenters, and laborers, as having careers is that the former, more typically than the latter, are trying to make the future different from the past—trying to create a new role rather than to play an old role well. The difference is obviously not hard and fast, since there are such things as hack poetry and creative dentistry. But the creative artist, in a wide sense that includes critics, scientists, and scholars, provides the paradigm case of a career whose conclusion leaves the world a bit different from what it used to be. If there is a connection between artistic freedom and creativity and the spirit of democracy, it is that the former provide examples of the kind of courageous self-transformation of which we hope democratic societies will become increasingly capable— transformation which is conscious and willed, rather than semiconsciously endured.

If, following Latour's and Descombes' suggestions, we were to start writing narratives of overlapping campaigns and careers which were not broken up into chapters with titles like "The Enlightenment," "Romanticism," "Literary Modernism," or "Late Capitalism," we would lose dramatic intensity. But we might help immunize ourselves against the passion of the infinite. If we dropped reference to movements, we could settle for telling a story about how the human beings in the neighborhood of the North Atlantic made their futures different from their pasts at a constantly accelerating pace. We could still, like Hegel and Acton, tell this story as a story of increasing freedom. But we could drop, along with any sense of inevitable progress, any sense of immanent teleology. We could drop any attempt to capitalize History, to view it as something as big and strong as Nature or God.

Such narratives of overlapping campaigns and careers would contain no hint that a career could be judged by its success in aligning itself with the movement of history. Both political and cultural history would be seen as a tissue of chances, mischances, and lost chances—a tissue from which, occasionally and briefly, beauty flashes forth, but to which sublimity is entirely irrelevant. It would not occur to somebody brought up on this kind of narrative to ask whether Joyce, Proust, Schönberg, Bartók, Picasso, and Matisse signified one of the major turnings in the cultural history of the West, or to ask whether that turning was perhaps not better signified by Rilke, Valéry, Strauss, Eliot, Klimt, and Heidegger. It would never occur to such a person to ask whether *Dissent* was central or marginal to the cultural or political life of its day. She would ask only whether *Dissent* did some good, whether it contributed to the success of some of the campaigns in which it took part. The answer to that question is clear.

Nor would it occur to her to ask whether Irving Howe's career had an overall cultural or political significance, or whether he had successfully synthesized his political and his literary aspirations. She would ask only whether his political conscience led him to support good causes, and whether his critical consciousness took the form of essays which stand comparison with those of Orwell and Wilson. The answers to those questions are equally obvious.

Irving Howe's good luck was as notable as his incredible energy and his exceptional honesty. Not only did he get when he was old what he had wished for when he was young, but he had no reason to regret his original wishes.

THE INSPIRATIONAL
VALUE OF GREAT WORKS
OF LITERATURE

Nil admirari prope res est una, Numici,
Solaque quae possit facere et servare beatum.

(*To stand in awe of nothing, Numicius,*
is practically the only way to feel really good about yourself.)

Horace, *Epistles*, I.vi.1–2

THE SELF-PROTECTIVE PROJECT described in this familiar Horatian tag is exemplified by one strain of thought in
Fredric Jameson's influential *Postmodernism, or The Cultural Logic
of Late Capitalism*. In one of the most depressing passages of that
profoundly antiromantic book, Jameson says that "the end
of the bourgeois ego, or monad, . . . means . . . the end . . . of
style, in the sense of the unique and the personal, the end of
the distinctive individual brush stroke."[1] Later he says that

> if the poststructuralist motif of the "death of the sub-
> ject" means anything socially, it signals the end of the

entrepreneurial and inner-directed individualism with its "charisma" and its accompanying categorial panoply of quaint romantic values such as that of the "genius" . . . Our social order is richer in information and more literate . . . This new order no longer needs prophets and seers of the high modernist and charismatic type, whether among its cultural products or its politicians. Such figures no longer hold any charm or magic for the subjects of a corporate, collectivized, post-individualistic age; in that case, goodbye to them without regret, as Brecht might have put it: woe to the country that needs geniuses, prophets, Great Writers, or demiurges![2]

Adoption of this line of thought produces what I shall call "knowingness." Knowingness is a state of soul which prevents shudders of awe. It makes one immune to romantic enthusiasm.

This state of soul is found in the teachers of literature in American colleges and universities who belong to what Harold Bloom calls the "School of Resentment." These people have learned from Jameson and others that they can no longer enjoy "the luxury of the old-fashioned ideological critique, the indignant moral denunciation of the other."[3] They have also learned that hero-worship is a sign of weakness, and a temptation to elitism. So they substitute Stoic endurance for both righteous anger and social hope. They substitute knowing theorization for awe, and resentment over the failures of the past for visions of a better future.

Although I prefer "knowingness" to Bloom's word "resentment," my view of these substitutions is pretty much the same as his. Bloom thinks that many rising young teachers of literature can ridicule anything but can hope for nothing, can explain everything but can idolize nothing. Bloom sees them as converting the study of literature into what he calls "one more dismal social science"—and thereby turning departments of literature into isolated academic backwaters. American sociology departments, which started out as movements for social reform, ended up training students to clothe statistics in jargon. If literature departments turn into departments of cultural studies, Bloom fears, they will start off hoping to do some badly needed political work, but will end up training their students to clothe resentment in jargon.

I think it is important to distinguish know-nothing criticisms of the contemporary American academy—the sort of thing you get from columnists like George Will and Jonathan Yardley, and politicians like William Bennett and Lynne Cheney—from the criticisms currently being offered by such insiders as Bloom and Christopher Ricks. The first set of critics believe everything they read in scandalmongering books by Dinesh D'Souza, David Lehman, and others. They do not read philosophy, but simply search out titles and sentences to which they can react with indignation. Much of their work belongs to the current conservative attempt to discredit the universities—which itself is part of a larger attempt to discredit all critics of the cynical oligarchy that has bought up the Republican Party. The insiders' criticism, on the other hand, has nothing to do with national politics. It comes from people who are careful readers, and whose loathing for the oligarchy is as great as Jameson's own.

I myself am neither a conservative nor an insider. Because my own disciplinary matrix is philosophy, I cannot entirely trust my sense of what is going on in literature departments. So I am never entirely sure whether Bloom's gloomy predictions are merely peevish, or whether he is more far-sighted than those who dismiss him as a petulant eccentric. But in the course of hanging around literature departments over the past decade or so, I have acquired some suspicions that parallel his.

The main reason I am prey to such suspicions is that I have watched, in the course of my lifetime, similarly gloomy predictions come true in my own discipline. Philosophers of my generation learned that an academic discipline can become almost unrecognizably different in a half-century—different, above all, in the sort of talents that get you tenure. A discipline can quite quickly start attracting a new sort of person, while becoming inhospitable to the kind of person it used to welcome.

Bloom is to Jameson as A. N. Whitehead was to A. J. Ayer in the 1930s. Whitehead stood for charisma, genius, romance, and Wordsworth. Like Bloom, he agreed with Goethe that the ability to shudder with awe is the best feature of human beings. Ayer, by contrast, stood for logic, debunking, and knowingness. He wanted philosophy to be a matter of scientific teamwork, rather than of imaginative breakthroughs by heroic figures. He saw theology, metaphysics, and literature as devoid of what he called "cognitive significance," and Whitehead as a good logician who had been ruined by poetry. Ayer regarded shudders of awe as neurotic symptoms. He helped create the philosophical tone which Iris Murdoch criticized in her celebrated essay "Against Dryness."

In the space of two generations, Ayer and dryness won out over Whitehead and romance. Philosophy in the English-speaking world became "analytic," antimetaphysical, unromantic, and highly professional. Analytic philosophy still attracts first-rate minds, but most of these minds are busy solving problems which no nonphilosopher recognizes as problems: problems which hook up with nothing outside the discipline.[4] So what goes on in anglophone philosophy departments has become largely invisible to the rest of the academy, and thus to the culture as a whole. This may be the fate that awaits literature departments.

Analytic philosophy is not exactly one more dismal social science, but its desire to be dryly scientific, and thereby to differentiate itself from the sloppy thinking it believes to be prevalent in literature departments, has made it stiff, awkward, and isolated. Those who admire this kind of philosophy often claim that philosophy professors are not only a lot drier but also a lot smarter nowadays than in the past. I do not think this is so. I think they are only a little meaner. Philosophy is now more adversarial and argumentative than it used to be, but I do not think that it is pursued at a higher intellectual level.

As philosophy became analytic, the reading habits of aspiring graduate students changed in a way that parallels recent changes in the habits of graduate students of literature. Fewer old books were read, and more recent articles. As early as the 1950s, philosophy students like myself who had, as undergraduates, been attracted to philosophy as a result of falling in love with Plato or Hegel or Whitehead, were dutifully writing Ph.D. dissertations on such Ayer-like topics as the proper analysis of subjunctive conditional sentences. This was, to be sure, an interesting problem. But it was clear to me that if I did not write on some such respectably analytic problem I would not get a very good job. Like the rest of my generation of philosophy Ph.D.'s, I was not exactly cynical, but I did know on which my side my bread was likely to be buttered. I am told, though I cannot vouch for the fact, that similar motives are often at work when today's graduate students of literature choose dissertation topics.

Nowadays, when analytic philosophers are asked to explain their cultural role and the value of their discipline, they typically fall back on the claim that the study of philosophy helps one see through pretentious, fuzzy thinking. So it does. The intellectual moves which the study of analytic philosophy trained me to make have proved very useful. Whenever, for example, I hear such words as "problematize" and "theorize," I reach for my analytic philosophy.

Still, prior to the rise of analytic philosophy, ridiculing pretentious fuzziness was only one of the things that philosophy professors did. Only some philosophers made this their specialty: Hobbes, Hume, and Bentham, for example, but not Spinoza, Hegel, T. H. Green, or Dewey. In the old days, there was another kind of philosopher—the romantic kind. This is the kind we do not get any more, at least in the English-speaking world. Undergraduates who want to grow up to be the next Hegel, Nietzsche, or Whitehead are not encouraged to go on for graduate work in anglophone philosophy departments. This is why my discipline has undergone both a paradigm shift and a personality change. Romance, genius, charisma, individual brush strokes, prophets, and demiurges have been out of style in anglophone philosophy for several generations. I doubt that they will ever come back into fashion, just as I doubt that American sociology departments will ever again be the centers of social activism they were in the early decades of the century.

So much for my analogy between the rise of cultural studies within English departments and of logical positivism within philosophy departments. I have no doubt that cultural studies will be as old hat thirty years from now as was logical positivism thirty years after its triumph. But the victory of logical positivism had irreversible effects on my discipline— it deprived it of romance and inspiration, and left only professional competence and intellectual sophistication. Familiarity with these effects makes me fear that Bloom may be right when he predicts that the victory of cultural studies would have irreversibly bad effects upon the study of literature.

To make clearer the bad effects I have in mind, let me explain what I mean by the term "inspirational value." I can do so most easily by citing an essay by the novelist Dorothy Allison: "Believing in Literature." There she describes what she calls her "atheist's religion"—a religion shaped, she says, by "literature" and by "her own dream of writing." Toward the close of this essay, she writes:

> There is a place where we are always alone with our own mortality, where we must simply have something greater than ourselves to hold onto—God or history or politics or literature or a belief in the healing power of love, or even righteous anger. Sometimes I think they are all the same. A reason to believe, a way to take the world by the throat and insist that there is more to this life than we have ever imagined.[5]

When I attribute inspirational value to works of literature, I mean that these works make people think there is more to this life than they ever imagined. This sort of effect is more often produced by Hegel or Marx than by Locke or Hume, Whitehead than Ayer, Wordsworth than Housman, Rilke than Brecht, Derrida than de Man, Bloom than Jameson.

Inspirational value is typically not produced by the operations of a method, a science, a discipline, or a profession. It is produced by the individual brush strokes of unprofessional prophets and demiurges. You cannot, for example, find inspirational value in a text at the same time that you are viewing it as the product of a mechanism of cultural production. To view a work in this way gives understanding but not hope, knowledge but not self-transformation. For knowledge is a matter of putting a work in a familiar context—relating it to things already known.

If it is to have inspirational value, a work must be allowed to recontexualize much of what you previously thought you knew; it cannot, at least at first, be itself recontextualized by what you already believe. Just as you cannot be swept off your feet by another human being at the same time that you recognize him or her as a good specimen of a certain type, so you cannot simultaneously be inspired by a work and be knowing about it. Later on—when first love has been replaced by marriage—you may acquire the ability to be both at once. But the really good marriages, the inspired marriages, are those which began in wild, unreflective infatuation.

A humanistic discipline is in good shape only when it produces both inspiring works and works which contextualize, and thereby deromanticize and debunk, those inspiring works. So I think philosophy, as an academic discipline, was in better shape when it had room for admirers of Whitehead as well as admirers of Ayer. I think that literature departments were in better shape when people of Bloom's and Allison's sort had a better chance than, I am told, they now have of being allowed to spend their teaching lives reiterating their idiosyncratic enthusiasms for their favorite prophets and demiurges. People of that sort are the ones Jameson thinks outdated, because they are still preoccupied with what he calls the "bourgeois ego." They are people whose motto is Wordsworth's "What we have loved/Others will love, and we will teach them how." This kind of teaching is different from the kind that produces knowingness, or technique, or professionalism.

Of course, if such connoisseurs of charisma were the only sort of teacher available, students would be short-changed. But they will also be short-changed if the only sort of teacher available is the knowing, debunking, nil admirari kind. We shall always need people in every discipline whose talents suit them for understanding rather than for hope, for placing a text in a context rather than celebrating its originality, and for detecting nonsense rather than producing it. But the natural tendency of professionalization and academicization is to favor a talent for analysis and problem-solving over imagination, to replace enthusiasm with dry, sardonic knowingness. The dismalness of a lot of social science, and of a lot of analytic philosophy, is evidence of what happens when this replacement is complete.

Within the academy, the humanities have been a refuge for enthusiasts. If there is no longer a place for them within either philosophy or literature departments, it is not clear where they will find shelter in the future. People like Bloom and Allison—people who began devouring books as soon as they learned to read, whose lives were saved by books—may get frozen out of those departments. If they are, the study of the humanities will continue to produce knowledge, but it may no longer produce hope. Humanistic education may become what it was in Oxbridge before the reforms of the 1870s: merely a turnstile for admission to the overclass.

I hope that I have made clear what I mean by "inspirational value." Now I should like to say something about the term "great works of literature." This term is often thought to be obsolete, because Platonism is obsolete. By "Platonism" I mean the idea that great works of literature all, in the end, say the same thing—and are great precisely because they do so. They inculcate the same eternal "humanistic" values. They remind us of the same immutable features of human experience. Platonism, in this sense, conflates inspiration and knowledge by saying that only the eternal inspires—that the source of greatness has always been out there, just behind the veil of appearances, and has been described many times before. The best a prophet or a demiurge can hope for is to say once again what has often been said, but to say it in a different way, to suit a different audience.

I agree that these Platonist assumptions are best discarded. But doing so should not lead us to discard the hope shared by Allison, Bloom, and Matthew Arnold—the hope for a religion of literature, in which works of the secular imagination replace Scripture as the principal source of inspiration and hope for each new generation. We should cheerfully admit that canons are temporary, and touchstones replaceable. But this should not lead us to discard the idea of greatness. We should see great works of literature as great because they have inspired many readers, not as having inspired many readers because they are great.

This difference may seem a quibble, but it is the whole difference between pragmatist functionalism and Platonist essentialism. For a functionalist, it is no surprise that some putatively great works leave some readers cold; functionalists do not expect the same key to open every heart. For functionalists like Bloom, the main reason for drawing up a literary canon, "ordering a lifetime's reading," is to be able to offer suggestions to the young about where they might find excitement and hope. Whereas essentialists take canonical status as indicating the presence of a link to eternal truth, and lack of interest in a canonical work as a moral flaw, functionalists take canonical status to be as changeable as the historical and personal situations of readers. Essentialist critics like de Man think that philosophy tells them how to read nonphilosophy. Functionalist critics like M. H. Abrams and Bloom read philosophical treatises in the same way they read poems—in search of excitement and hope.

The Platonist subordination of time to eternity, and of hope and inspiration to knowledge, produces the attitude which Mark Edmundson criticizes in his Literature against Philosophy: Plato to Derrida. "To the degree that your terminology claims to encompass a text, to know it better than it knows itself," Edmundson says, "to that degree you give up the possibility of being read by it."[6] Edmundson's target is the assumption that one's reading is insufficiently informed if one is unable to put the text one is reading within a previously formulated theoretical context—a context which enables one, in the manner of Jameson, to treat the latest birth of time as just another specimen, reiterating a known type.

It is this assumption against which Shelley, in his Defence of Poetry, protested. "Poets," he said, "are the hierophants of an unapprehended inspiration; the mirrors of the gigantic shadows which futurity casts upon the present." There was, to be sure, still plenty of Platonism in Shelley, even more than there was in Arnold. But, since Shelley's day, there has been less Platonism in every succeeding generation, thanks to figures like Marx, Whitman, and Dewey—romantic utopians who prophesied a human future which would be patterned neither on the past nor on the eternal.

Though I think of Derrida as just such a romantic utopian, I cannot interpret either Foucault or Jameson in this way. I think that Bloom is right when he refers to the present "odd blend of Foucault and Marx" as "a very minor episode in the endless history of Platonism"—the endless attempt to make the intellect sovereign over the imagination.[7] Edmundson seems to me right in describing much of what is going on in anglophone literature departments as part of the latest attempt by knowing philosophers to gain supremacy over inspired poets. I hope that the philosophers never succeed in this attempt. But I do not think that literature will succeed in resisting philosophy unless literary critics think of it as Bloom does: as having nothing to do with eternity, knowledge, or stability, and everything to do with futurity and hope—with taking the world by the throat and insisting that there is more to this life than we have ever imagined.

Unfortunately, in contemporary American academic culture, it is commonly assumed that once you have seen through Plato, essentialism, and eternal truth you will naturally turn to Marx. The attempt to take the world by the throat is still, in the minds of Jameson and his admirers, associated with Marxism. This association seems to me merely quaint, as does Jameson's use of the term "late capitalism"—a term which equivocates nicely between economic history and millenarian hope. The main thing contemporary academic Marxists inherit from Marx and Engels is the conviction that the quest for the cooperative commonwealth should be scientific rather than utopian, knowing rather than romantic.

This conviction seems to me entirely mistaken. I take Foucault's refusal to indulge in utopian thinking not as sagacity but as a result of his unfortunate inability to believe in the possibility of human happiness, and his consequent inability to think of beauty as the promise of happiness. Attempts to imitate Foucault make it hard for his followers to take poets like Blake or Whitman seriously. So it is hard for these followers to take seriously people inspired by such poets—people like Jean Jaurès, Eugene Debs, Vaclav Havel, and Bill Bradley. The Foucauldian academic Left in contemporary America is exactly the sort of Left that the oligarchy dreams of: a Left whose members are so busy unmasking the present that they have no time to discuss what laws need to be passed in order to create a better future.

Emerson famously distinguished between the party of memory and the party of hope. Bloom has remarked that this distinction is now, in its application to American academic politics, out of date: the party of memory, he says, is the party of hope. His point is that, among students of literature, it is only those who agree with Hölderlin that "what abides was founded by poets" who are still capable of social hope. I suspect he is right at least to this extent: it is only those who still read for inspiration who are likely to be of much use in building a cooperative commonwealth. So I do not see the disagreement between Jamesonians and Bloomians as a disagreement between those who take politics seriously and those who do not. Instead, I see it as between people taking refuge in self-protective knowingness about the present and romantic utopians trying to imagine a better future.

NOTES

AMERICAN NATIONAL PRIDE

1. One particularly good example of such purchase is the Senate's vote for an ad hoc change in the law so as to hinder the Teamsters Union from organizing the Federal Express Company. See the debate on this matter initiated by Senator Edward Kennedy's speech (*Congressional Record*, October 1, 1996, pp. S12097ff.), especially Senator Paul Simon's remarks: "I think we have to honestly ask ourselves, why is Federal Express being given preferential treatment in this body now? I think the honest answer is Federal Express has been very generous in their campaign contributions" (p. S12106). After the Senate had voted in the company's favor, a spokesman for Federal Express was quoted as saying, "We played political hardball, and we won."

2. William James, "The Social Value of the College-Bred," in James, *Essays, Comments, and Reviews* (Cambridge, Mass.: Harvard University Press, 1987), p. 109.

3. Herbert Croly, *The Promise of American Life* (New York: Capricorn Books, 1964; orig. pub. 1909), p. 1.

4. James Baldwin, *The Fire Next Time* (New York: Dell, 1988; orig. pub. 1963), p. 5.

5. Ibid., p. 98.

6. Ibid., p. 97.

7. Nelson Lichtenstein, *The Most Dangerous Man in Detroit: Walter Reuther and the Fate of American Labor* (New York: Basic Books, 1994), p. 383.

8. I use "secularism" in the sense of "anticlericalism" rather than of "atheism." Dewey's dislike of "aggressive atheism" is made clear in *A Common Faith*. I have argued elsewhere that Dewey, like James, wanted pragmatism to be compatible with religious belief—but only with a privatized religious belief, not with the sort of religious belief that produces churches, especially churches which take political positions. See Rorty, "Religious Faith, Intellectual Responsibility, and Romance," in Ruth-Anna Putnam, ed., *The Cambridge Companion to William James* (Cambridge: Cambridge University Press, 1997); idem, "Pragmatism as Romantic Polytheism," in Morris Dickstein, ed., *The New Pragmatism* (Durham, N.C.: Duke University Press, 1998); idem, "Religion as Conversation-Stopper," *Common Knowledge* 3 (Spring 1994): 1–6. This last is a reply to Stephen Carter's argument that religious voices should be heard in the public square.

9. *Leaves of Grass*, p. 85. All references to both *Leaves of Grass* and *Democratic Vistas* are to Walt Whitman, *Complete Poetry and Selected Prose* (New York: Library of America, 1982).

10. Kenneth Rexroth, "Walt Whitman," *Saturday Review* 3 (September 1966), reprinted in Graham Clarke, ed., *Walt Whitman: Critical Assessments*, vol. 3 (New York: Routledge, 1994), p. 241.

11. Whitman, *Democratic Vistas*, p. 930.

12. John Dewey, "Maeterlinck's Philosophy of Life," in *The Middle Works of John Dewey*, vol. 6 (Carbondale: Southern Illinois University Press, 1978), p. 135. Dewey says that Emerson, Whitman, and Maeterlinck are the only three to have grasped this fact about democracy. Dewey's term "metaphysic" is a bit unfortunate. He might have expressed his meaning better by saying that, Nietzsche to the contrary, democracy is the principal means by which a more evolved form of humanity will come into existence.

Kenneth Burke once wrote (*A Grammar of Motives*, p. 504) that "characters possess *degrees of being* in proportion to the variety of perspectives from which they can with justice be perceived. Thus we could say that plants have 'less being' than animals, because each higher order admits and requires a new dimension of terms not literally relevant to the lower orders." Democratic humanity, Dewey and Burke might have agreed, has "more being" than predemocratic humanity. The citizens of a democratic, Whitmanesque society are able to create new, hitherto unimagined roles and goals for themselves. So a greater variety of perspectives, and of descriptive terms, becomes available to them, and can with justice be used to account for them.

13. Steven Rockefeller, *John Dewey: Religious Faith and Democratic Humanism* (New York: Columbia University Press, 1991), p. 4.

14. Whitman, *Democratic Vistas*, p. 960.

15. Whitman, *Notebooks and Unpublished Prose Manuscripts*, in Whitman, *Collected Writings*, vol. 6, ed. Edward F. Grier (New York: New York University Press, 1984), p. 2011. See pp. 2007–2008 for helpful editorial notes and references to secondary material which discusses the extent of Whitman's reading in Hegel, and the nature of Hegel's influence on him. He seems to have read only as much Hegel as was translated by Frederic Hedge in his 1847 book, *German Prose Writers*—mainly the Introduction to the *Lectures on the Philosophy of History*—as well as an intelligent five-page summary of Hegel's system by Joseph Gostick.

16. Whitman, *Notebooks and Unpublished Prose Manuscripts*, p. 2012.

17. Hegel, *Lectures on the Philosophy of World-History: Introduction—Reason in History*, trans. H. B. Nisbet (Cambridge: Cambridge University Press, 1975), pp. 170–171.

18. "Carlyle from American Points of View," in Whitman, *Prose Works* (Philadelphia: David McKay, 1900), p. 171.

19. Whitman, *Leaves of Grass*, p. 16.

20. Ibid., p. 5.

21. Ibid., p. 71.

22. Whitman, *Democratic Vistas*, p. 930.

23. Ibid., p. 929.

24. Whitman hoped that the Era of Reconstruction would be the birth of such a new culture. See David S. Reynolds, *Walt Whitman's America: A Cultural Biography* (New York: Random House, 1995), ch. 14.

25. See Avishai Margalit, *The Decent Society* (Cambridge, Mass.: Harvard University Press, 1996), p. 1.

26. I am indebted to Mark Edmundson for this point about the somewhat unbalanced historiography of the Sixties.

27. For an account of the importance of rock-and-roll to the Sixties, see the chapter "Zappa and Havel" in Paul Berman's *A Tale of Two Utopias: The Political Journey of the Generation of 1968* (New York: Norton, 1996).

28. Whitman, *Leaves of Grass*, p. 23.

29. Ibid., p. 50.

30. Ibid., p. 56.

31. "Creative Democracy—The Task before Us," in *Later Works of John Dewey*, vol. 14 (Carbondale: Southern Illinois University Press, 1988), p. 229.

32. Whitman, *Democratic Vistas*, p. 956.

33. Baldwin, *The Fire Next Time*, p. 101.

34. See the title essay in Sidney Hook, *Pragmatism and the Tragic Sense of Life* (New York: Basic Books, 1974).

35. For an account of Niebuhr's criticisms of Dewey, see Daniel F. Rice, *Reinhold Niebuhr and John Dewey: An American Odyssey* (Albany: SUNY Press, 1993). For a recent admiring treatment of Niebuhr (and of Henry Adams), see John Patrick Diggins, *The Promise of Pragmatism* (Chicago: University of Chicago Press, 1994). For Elshtain's restatement of Augustine, see her *Augustine and the Limits of Politics* (Notre Dame: Notre Dame University Press, 1995); for Delbanco's, see his book *The Death of Satan: How Americans Have Lost the Sense of Evil* (New York: Farrar, Straus and Giroux, 1995).

36. Delbanco, *The Death of Satan*, pp. 175–176.

37. *Spectare* is the Latin translation of the Greek verb *theorein*. Both words mean "to look at."

THE ECLIPSE OF THE REFORMIST LEFT

1. See David Remnick, "The First and the Last: Lenin Revealed, and Buried by Gorbachev," *New Yorker*, November 18, 1996, pp. 118–122.

2. Marxists usually do not want to count Whitman, Dewey, and FDR as men of the Left. But since Dewey despaired of capitalism during

the Depression, some of his Marxisant admirers regard him as having crossed the crucial bridge in his later years. I cannot see the point of using such despair as a litmus test for authentic leftiness.

3. See, for example, the fifth chapter of Christopher Phelps's *Young Sidney Hook: Marxist and Pragmatist* (Ithaca: Cornell University Press, 1997). After giving a sympathetic account of Hook's career up to 1938, Phelps finds himself unable to forgive the fact that from then on Hook was "in retreat from revolution and increasingly aligned with social democracy, barely distinguished from liberal reformism in the degree of compromise with capitalist institutions he was willing to accept" (p. 199).

4. Herbert Croly, *The Promise of American Life* (New York: Capricorn Books, 1964; orig. pub. 1909), p. 22.

5. Ibid., p. 14.

6. Ibid., p. 25.

7. Ibid., p. 23.

8. Ibid., p. 139.

9. Richard T. Ely, *Social Aspects of Christianity* (New York: Thomas Y. Crowell, 1889), p. 143.

10. Ibid., p. 137.

11. Eldon Eisenach, *The Lost Promise of Progressivism* (Lawrence: University Press of Kansas, 1994), p. 3. There is an ironic contrast between the Progressives' denial that the individual freedom guaranteed by the Constitution is the central American value and Jürgen Habermas' claim (the title of his much-discussed article of 1989) that "the only sort of patriotism that will not alienate us from the West is constitutional patriotism [*Verfassungspatriotismus*]" (*Die Zeit*, July 11, 1989). Habermas was arguing against a revival of an older variety of German national pride, and urging that the only sort of national pride appropriate for Germany was pride in the freedoms embedded in the postwar German *Grundgesetz*. The Progressives were arguing that the U.S. Constitution was being used as an excuse for perpetuating inequality (by the Supreme Court majority in the *Lochner* decision, for example—a decision which struck down protection for workers in the name of freedom of contract).

The moral of the contrast is that what constitutes proper national pride is always going to be contested between Left and Right, and that such arguments will always turn on particular contingencies in the lives of individual nations.

12. Eisenach, The Lost Promise of Progressivism, p. 7.

13. See George S. McGovern and Leonard F. Guttridge, The Great Coalfield War (Boston: Houghton Mifflin, 1972)—an account of the wave of strikes which swept the mines of Colorado in 1913–1914.

14. Daniel Bell, Marxian Socialism in the United States (Ithaca: Cornell University Press, 1996), p. 45.

15. On these photographs, see Nelson Lichtenstein, The Most Dangerous Man in Detroit: Walter Reuther and the Fate of American Labor (New York: Basic Books, 1994), p. 85 (also p. 237, on the role of Henry Luce's magazines in obtaining respectability for the labor unions).

16. Todd Gitlin, The Sixties: Years of Hope, Days of Rage (New York: Bantam Books, 1987), p. 178.

17. Ibid., p. 162.

18. Historians who like to pick out the exact moment of metamorphosis should consider the account (by one of the Berkeley protesters, reminiscing in the documentary Berkeley in the Sixties) of what happened on the day after the students had been prevented, by troops mounted on armored personnel carriers, from closing down the Induction Center in Oakland. The students, having no better idea of what to do the next day, returned to the center (now closed for the weekend), sat down in the street, and began to sing. At a certain point their song changed from "Solidarity Forever" to "We All Live in a Yellow Submarine." That may have been the moment at which an activist political Left began to be replaced by a spectatorial, cultural Left.

19. These people think that in the Third World Marxism is still indispensable. They hope that Marxist movements can, by internal reform, survive the opening of the Lubyanka Prison, just as Roman Catholicism managed, by internal reform, to survive the opening of the dungeons of Toledo. They could be right, but I doubt it.

20. C. Wright Mills, quoted in Christopher Lasch, The New Radicalism in America (New York: Random House, 1965), p. 298.

21. Walter Rauschenbusch, *Prayers of the Social Awakening* (Boston: Pilgrim Press, 1909), p. 101.

22. For a description of this party, see Sam Tanenhaus, *Whittaker Chambers: A Biography* (New York: Random House, 1997), pp. 141–142.

23. Christopher Lasch, *The Agony of the American Left* (New York: Vintage, 1969), p. viii.

24. Ibid., p. 10.

25. Ibid., p. 29.

26. Ibid., p. 27.

27. On the role of anti-Communism in splitting the left in the early Sixties, see Paul Berman, *A Tale of Two Utopias: The Political Journey of the Generation of 1968* (New York: Norton, 1996), pp. 63–83.

28. See Lichtenstein, *The Most Dangerous Man in Detroit*, pp. 392–395.

29. Berman, *A Tale of Two Utopias*, p. 8.

A CULTURAL LEFT

1. Just as linguists joke that a language is a dialect that has an army and a navy, one might joke that an identity group is an interest group that boasts an academic program. But there is, of course, a reason not all interest groups count as identity groups: you can move into and out of an interest group (the professoriat, the unemployed), but the sadism of your neighbors may not let you move out of an identity group. See Joseph Raz and Avishai Margalit, "National Self-Determination," *Journal of Philosophy* 87 (September 1990): 439–461, for a list of six characteristics that give a group an "identity" in the relevant sense. See also idem, "Liberalism and the Right to Culture," *Social Research* 21, no. 3 (Fall 1994): 491–510.

2. Here I use Margalit's definition of "civilized society": a society in which individuals do not humiliate one another. See Chapter 1, n. 25, above.

3. For an account of a family trying to get by at this income level, see Susan Sheehan, "Ain't No Middle Class," *New Yorker*, December 11, 1995, pp. 82–93.

4. *New York Times*, March 3, 1996, p. 28.

5. Many of these conferences concern the tragic effects of globalization on cultural identity. See Richard Rorty, "Global Utopias, History and Philosophy," in Luiz Soares, ed., *Cultural Pluralism, Identity, and Globalization* (Rio de Janeiro: UNESCO/ISSC/EDUCAM, 1996), pp. 457–469. This volume contains the proceedings of a UNESCO conference that was held in a room overlooking the beaches of Copacabana.

6. See Karen Arenson, "Cuts in Tuition Assistance Put College beyond Reach of Poorest Students," *New York Times*, January 27, 1997, p. B1, reporting on a study by Thomas G. Mortenson for the National Council of Educational Opportunity Associations: "Mr. Mortenson has found that the proportion of students earning college degrees by age twenty-four from families in the richest quarter of the population (in 1994, those with incomes above $60,000) has jumped sharply, to 79 percent in 1994 from 31 percent in 1979. But the rate among students from families in the poorest population (with 1994 incomes below $22,000) stayed flat over the same years, at about 8 percent."

7. Daniel Bell is right when he says, in an article subtitled "Middle Class Fears Turn Class Wars into Culture Wars," that there has been a "shift from economics to culture in defining the divisions in society." See Daniel Bell, "The Disunited States of America," *Times Literary Supplement*, June 9, 1995, p. 16. The academic Left and the "conservative intellectuals" (e.g., the editorialists for the *Wall Street Journal*) have collaborated in bringing about this shift.

8. The clash between these two responses was well illustrated at a "Teach-In for Labor" held at Columbia University on October 3–4, 1996. Orlando Patterson, the eminent historian of slavery, argued that the border with Mexico would sooner or later have to be closed to protect American workers. He was heckled by people shouting, "What about the workers in the Third World?" Black scholars do not often get booed by predominantly white and leftist audiences, but it happened this time. I suspect that the issue Patterson raised will be the most deeply divisive that the American Left will face in the twenty-first century. I

wish that I had some good ideas about how the dilemma might be resolved, but I do not.

9. John Dewey, *Reconstruction in Philosophy*, in *The Middle Works of John Dewey*, vol. 12 (Carbondale: Southern Illinois University Press, 1982), pp. 187–188.

10. Mark Edmundson, *Nightmare on Main Street: Angels, Sadomasochism, and the Culture of the Gothic* (Cambridge, Mass.: Harvard University Press, 1997), p. 41.

11. Ibid., p. 42.

12. For a good example of the conventional wisdom of the cultural Left on this topic, see Bill Readings, *The University in Ruins* (Cambridge, Mass.: Harvard University Press, 1996), ch. 3, "The Decline of the Nation-State." The passage quoted is on p. 43. Readings goes on to speak of "the hollowing out of political subjectivity that accompanies the decline of the nation-state" (p. 48), but he does not deplore this hollowing out or hope that the process may be reversed. I do both.

13. For an account of America which draws on Baudrillard, see Fred M. Dolan, *Allegories of America* (Ithaca: Cornell University Press, 1994), esp. pp. 60–73, the opening pages of a chapter called "Cold War Metaphysics." One would never guess, from Dolan's account, that there might have been a real, nonmetaphysical, nonimaginary point to fighting the Cold War.

14. The first item on such a list would obviously be truly radical reform of campaign financing—the issue on which there is, at present, the greatest unanimity among American voters. Everybody knows that nothing much will change in America as long as the votes of our legislators can be bought, and that those accustomed to buying those votes will fight like tigers against public financing of campaigns: our legislators will be bribed to continue letting themselves be bribed.

15. For a more favorable view of the chances of participatory democracy, see Robert Westbrook, *John Dewey and American Democracy* (Ithaca: Cornell University Press, 1991), esp. pp. 300–318 (a discussion of Dewey's response to Lippmann) and pp. 537–552 (a summary of Dewey's position, and criticism of my own reading of Dewey).

MOVEMENTS AND CAMPAIGNS

1. Irving Howe, "This Age of Conformity," in Howe, *Selected Writings, 1950–1990* (San Diego: Harcourt Brace, 1990), p. 46.

2. Irving Howe, *A Margin of Hope: An Intellectual Autobiography* (San Diego: Harcourt Brace Jovanovich, 1982), p. 160.

3. Ibid., p. 121.

4. Ibid., p. 150.

5. Irving Howe, *Politics and the Novel* (New York: New American Library, 1987; orig. pub. 1957), Epilogue, p. 254. Howe takes the phrase from an anonymous contemporary of Dostoevsky's.

6. Howe, *A Margin of Hope*, pp. 194–195.

7. Ibid., p. 337.

8. Howe, *Politics and the Novel*, p. 23.

9. See Harold Bloom, *Agon* (Oxford: Oxford University Press, 1982), p. 35.

10. Howe, *Selected Writings, 1950–1990*, p. 141.

11. Ibid., p. 165.

THE INSPIRATIONAL VALUE OF GREAT WORKS OF LITERATURE

1. Fredric Jameson, *Postmodernism, or The Cultural Logic of Late Capitalism* (Durham, N.C.: Duke University Press, 1991), p. 15.

2. Ibid., p. 306.

3. Jameson, *Postmodernism*, p. 46.

4. The best of these minds, however, are more inclined to dissolve problems than to solve them. They challenge the presuppositions of the problems with which the profession is currently occupied. This is what Ludwig Wittgenstein did in his *Philosophical Investigations*, and similar challenges are found in the work of the contemporary analytic philosophers I most admire—for example, Annette Baier, Donald Davidson, and Daniel Dennett. Such innovators are always viewed with some suspicion: those brought up on the old problems would like to think that

their clever solutions to those problems are permanent contributions to human knowledge. Forty-odd years after its publication, *Philosophical Investigations* still makes many philosophers nervous. They view Wittgenstein as a spoilsport.

5. Dorothy Allison, "Believing in Literature," in Allison, *Skin: Talking about Sex, Class, and Literature* (Ithaca, N.Y.: Firebrand Books, 1994), p. 181.

6. Mark Edmundson, *Literature against Philosophy: Plato to Derrida* (New York: Cambridge University Press, 1995), p. 128.

7. Harold Bloom, *The Western Canon: The Books and School of the Ages* (New York: Harcourt Brace, 1994), p. 18. Unfortunately, Bloom attributes this latest version of Platonism to "our current New Historicists." I think it is absent from the work of Stephen Greenblatt, who is too good a critic to be buffaloed by theory. But lesser Foucauldians do indeed think of Foucault and Marx as providing keys sufficient to unlock any text.

ACKNOWLEDGMENTS

THESE LECTURES were written over the course of seven months in 1996–1997, months in which I enjoyed the hospitality of the Stanford Humanities Center—a perfect place for uninterrupted reading and writing. I am grateful to the staff of the Center for making everything so smooth and easy for me, and to my fellow Fellows for good conversation and for useful criticisms of my philosophical and political views.

I sent drafts of the lectures to several friends and colleagues for comment. I greatly appreciate the time and effort which Mark Edmundson, J. C. Levenson, Daryl Levinson, Nelson Lichtenstein, Derek Nystrom, Jay Rorty, Mary Rorty, Lindsay Waters, and Robert Westbrook devoted to reading through these drafts and to making suggestions about how they might be improved. I probably should have accepted more of their suggestions than I did.

For this volume, I have supplemented my three Massey Lectures with two talks given on earlier occasions, hoping that these appendixes may render more plausible, or at least clarify, some of the things I say in the body of the book.

"Movements and Campaigns" was delivered at a colloquium held in memory of Irving Howe at the Graduate Center of the City University of New York. A shortened version was subsequently published in *Dissent* (Winter 1995: 55–60), to whose editors I am grateful for permission to reprint.

"The Inspirational Value of Great Works of Literature" was delivered at the annual meeting of the Modern Language Association of America in December 1995. In it, I express some fears for the future of the literature departments in our universities—the departments whose teachers and students make up the core of what I call the "cultural Left." It was subsequently printed in *Raritan* 16 (Summer 1996: 8–17). I appreciate the permission given by *Raritan*'s editor, Richard Poirier, to include a slightly revised version in this volume.

I should like to thank Maria Ascher, Ana Mitric, and Mike Millner for very helpful assistance in putting together the final version of the manuscript.

INDEX